.the.
divine
INTERCESSOR

PURSUING INTERCESSION
AND INTIMACY WITH JESUS

GARY WILKERSON

The Divine Intercessor

Published by
David Wilkerson Publications, Inc.
P. O. Box 260
Lindale, TX 75771

ISBN 0-97-9326-2-6

Edited by Carol B. Patterson

Foreword

When I first read my son's manuscript on prayer, I knew right away that the Holy Spirit had given him an open heaven and a powerful message that would motivate multitudes to pray.

The impact *The Divine Intercessor* had on me was immediate and demanded a response—*I wanted to pray!* I wanted to spend more time with the Lord, not motivated by a legal responsibility, but by a love impulse.

Gary has taken the mystery out of prayer. He leads us to Christ himself and the uncomplicated life of prayer He exemplifies. This is certainly not a "how to" book, but rather a "want to" book. You will want to pray as you read.

Gary is a man of prayer. What he has shared is a fresh revelation given him while on his knees. He knows both the joy and anguish of those who have set their hearts to seek the Lord with their whole heart.

You would not be reading this book if you did not have a desire to develop a life of prayer. May the Holy Spirit use it to awaken and inspire you to pray as you've never prayed before.

David Wilkerson

Dedication

To my wife Kelly and my kids, Ashley,
Evan, Elliot and Annie.
To my mom and dad and brother and
sisters—who all show
the tenderness of intimacy and the zeal
of intercession.

Acknowledgements

Special thanks to Cheryl Jones, Mike Colchin and Carol Patterson for their fine work on the manuscript.

Introduction

Jesus longs for a people who seek His face and His hand with passion—His face for intimacy and His hand for His mighty works on the earth. These two elements of prayer, intimacy and intercession, go hand in hand. According to Daniel 11:32, it is the "people who know their God" that will "be strong and do exploits."

No man can truly know the works of God's hand without first having spent a long time in the shadows seeking His face. When I was nineteen God spoke to my heart and offered me a choice: "Will you spend your life seeking my hand or my face?" I chose to seek His face. I chose intimacy—the secret place with God. It has not always been easy and many times I wanted to change my answer. I often wondered, "Couldn't I accomplish more, build more, and make a greater impact on the world if I just wanted His hand to move in might on the earth?" Looking back, I see the reason Jesus led me to choose to seek His face, for it is truly out of this place that God can work His most precious plans through a person.

The heart of Jesus, the Divine Intercessor, was constantly seeking the face and hand of His Father while He was on earth. He wants this to be a way of life for us, as well, so He left an example of prayer for us to follow. However, it is not a study of methods or "ten steps…" or rote prayer, but something much more practical. He not only wants us to pray *to* Him but *with* Him.

Jesus aids and encourages us, and endows us with spiritual power and authority. With this empowerment, we are to seek His face and His hand. Seek intimacy with Him *that you might know and love Him*, and intercession *that the world may be touched by the very hand of God.*

Table of Contents

The Divine Intercessor

And it came to pass, that, as he was praying in a certain place, when he ceased, one of his disciples said unto him, Lord, teach us to pray, as John also taught his disciples. And he said unto them, When ye pray, say, Our Father which art in heaven, Hallowed be thy name. Thy kingdom come. Thy will be done, as in heaven, so in earth. Give us day by day our daily bread. And forgive us our sins; for we also forgive every one that is indebted to us. And lead us not into temptation; but deliver us from evil.

And he said unto them, Which of you shall have a friend, and shall go unto him at midnight, and say unto him, Friend, lend me three loaves; For a friend of mine in his journey is come to me, and I have nothing to set before him? And he from within shall answer and say, Trouble me not: the door is now shut, and my children are with me in bed; I cannot rise and give thee. I say unto you, Though he will not rise and give him, because he is his friend, yet

> *because of his importunity he will rise and give him as many as he needeth. And I say unto you, Ask, and it shall be given you; seek, and ye shall find; knock, and it shall be opened unto you (Luke 11:1-9 KJV).*

Far too many of us attend prayerless churches led by prayerless pastors, who are working with prayerless elders and deacons. We hear well-crafted and theologically correct sermons that are brought to the pulpit after a week of prayerless sermon preparation. Yet we have no right to grumble. We sit in pews as prayerless people leading prayerless lives in a world that is in desperate need of *extravagant prayer.*

It was prayer that stirred the disciples to ask boldly of Jesus, "Teach us to pray." They heard Jesus teach but did not ask Him to teach them *to teach.* They saw the miracles Jesus performed but did not ask Him to teach them *to heal*—they asked Him to teach them *to PRAY.*

This generation seems to be requesting: "Lord, make me a great, gifted and articulate teacher. God, give me healing power." These are fine desires but we are less inclined to ask what these friends of Jesus were asking, "Teach us to pray." I believe they made this request because they were standing in the presence of and listening to the fiery, passionate prayers of Jesus, the Divine Intercessor. If we could have stood and heard what they heard, I have no doubt that our passion would have been equally stirred.

The familiar passage in Luke 11 is commonly known

as The Lord's Prayer. A few years ago in some parts of this country, it was customary for spectators at high school football games to recite The Lord's Prayer out loud together before the start of the game. The Lord's Prayer is ingrained in our society and most church members know it well. In early childhood, we learn to recite, "*Our Father, which art in heaven, hallowed be thy name.*" It is almost a spiritual national anthem.

Even though most people are familiar with this passage, few are aware that it teaches more than the mere reciting of a memorized prayer. A closer study shows us something deeper, something intriguing and valuable, something beyond just the words of The Lord's Prayer. Jesus relates this implicit deeper message in a parable to His disciples. He longs for His bride to desire to learn to walk in a life of extravagant, passionate prayer. He not only gives us a language for prayer, but He instills in us a burning passion to seek the heart of the Father.

As He Was Praying

As the disciples journeyed with Jesus, they noticed that He prayed frequently. It was not uncommon for Him to pray for long periods of time in the morning before sunrise. Sometimes He spent all day in prayer; at other times He prayed all night. He was what the Scriptures call "an intercessor." He interceded, *which means He stood between God and man* to bring forth on earth blessings from heaven. While He was on earth, He was the Divine Intercessor, God among us, interceding on our behalf. He loved to intercede.

When His disciples heard Jesus praying, they were intrigued. Their emotions and spiritual passions stirred within them. Their slumbering spirits were quickened and awakened and they wanted to have what Jesus had. They waited until Jesus finished His praying before they asked Him to teach them to pray (Luke 1:1). They did not wait just a few minutes for His prayer to end, because Jesus usually prayed for hours at a time. His praying was not the quick recitation of a memorized prayer. He was not kneeling by a rock saying, "Our Father, which art in heaven…[quickly running through the prayer]…amen!" No, they heard Jesus praying as the Divine Intercessor. It was a prayer unlike any they had ever heard before. He prayed *with authority.*

Earlier the disciples had heard Jesus teach for the first time. Afterward they came up to Him and said, "We have never heard such teaching in our life. You have authority like we have never heard before. The Pharisees don't teach like that. Our schoolteachers don't teach like that. Our religious leaders don't teach like that. Jesus, you have authority when you speak the Word." They observed the same thing when they heard Him praying. They lost all interest in merely repeating religious jargon—they desperately wanted what Jesus had.

Why did the disciples of Jesus so desperately want to learn to pray like He prayed? They had all been brought up in the traditional religious, Jewish customs of the day, and they had prayed from the time they were little children. The Old Testament taught them certain prayers—morning prayers, noon prayers, and evening prayers. They prayed for their families, their nation, and their leaders.

They had specific types of prayers for different seasons and holy days. In other words, they were men steeped in the *tradition of prayer.*

Many of the disciples had been taught by John the Baptist and I don't believe he was a timid pray-er. I'm certain he didn't just throw out tiny prayers every once in a while. No, when John the Baptist prayed, he probably looked like a raving maniac by modern American standards. He was passionate about the kingdom of God coming to earth. His prayers must have been revolutionary compared to the traditional prayers that the disciples had learned in the temple and the prayers taught by the Pharisees. But even though the disciples learned about passionate prayer from John, they still felt totally inadequate in prayer after hearing Jesus pray. The cry of their hearts was, "We don't know a thing about prayer. We've prayed the synagogue prayers and we've learned much from John, but we now see that we know nothing compared to what you have. *Jesus, teach us to pray."*

Let me invite you into something that you may never have experienced before in your life. I invite you into the presence of Jesus. Come sit at His feet and begin to know Him. Come wait on Him. Spend hours, if you will, in His presence saying, "Lord Jesus, I do not know how to pray. Here I am. I offer my life to you. I know nothing about prayer, but I want to learn." Learning about prayer through books, tapes, seminars or sermons can be helpful, just as John's modeling of prayer helped the disciples. But that is not enough. Learning from John paled in comparison to what they were now hearing in Jesus' prayers. They were forever spoiled, ruined. The old school would never again satisfy. It was going to be "Pray like Jesus or never pray again."

When I first started learning to pray, I read an instruction manual on how to pray for one hour. I thought I would have no problem spending an hour in prayer. I figured that since I was going to spend my life as a pastor, I should probably get accustomed to praying, so I studied the techniques of prayer presented in this workbook. I also read the biographical books of great men of prayer such as Rees Howell and John Hyde. Rees Howell commonly spent eight hours a day in prayer. His reputation spread and he became known as "Rees Howell, Intercessor" because of the duration and spiritual intensity of his prayers. John Hyde was another well-known man of prayer. He often prayed five to seven hours per day, and his propensity for praying gained him the nickname "Praying Hyde."

After studying the manual of prayer techniques and reading the biographies of famous pray-ers, I decided (at the age of sixteen!) that I was equipped to be a renowned intercessor. I thought I should start my career as an intercessor by praying for one full hour, so I set my alarm clock and began.

"Oh, God, I thank you that I am going to be like Rees Howell, Intercessor. I will be known as Gary Wilkerson, Intercessor, or maybe Praying Wilkerson. Thank you for helping me learn to pray." I looked over at the clock and only 15 seconds had ticked off.

"Just 59 minutes and 45 seconds left, Lord, and I will have accomplished what even your disciples could not do. They fell asleep in less than an hour and I will stand here with you." That took another 30 seconds.

I prayed for my family and for the food that I would eat later in the day. Only 45 seconds had gone by and already I could think of nothing else to pray for.

It crossed my mind that I could pray for the nations, so I confidently started out, "Lord, bless China. Bless England. Bless France, Romania, and Argentina." That took about two or three minutes—and then I exhausted my knowledge of geography. I mentioned every nation I could think of and only three minutes had passed.

I put the book down, got into my car and went to the Christian bookstore to find some books on great evangelists. You see, it had taken only three or four minutes for me to come to the conclusion that I was just not suited for prayer. No, I knew I was an action kind of guy—rambunctious like John the Baptist—who needed to make things happen! None of this whiling away my time with I-love-you-Jesus kind of prayers. So my career as a man-of-prayer/intercessor came to an abrupt and unceremonious end.

It is a tragedy that oftentimes we give up on prayer so easily. Many of us try to become great men and women of prayer, great and effective intercessors, and we dive into it with passion. "Lord, I want to give my heart. I want to know how to pray. I want to seek your face. There are so many needs and so many desperate cries. I need to learn how to pray—Lord, teach me to pray!"

Many of us need to forget our preconceived ideas about prayer and see the model of passion, power, and authority in the prayer of the Divine Intercessor, Jesus Christ. He is the One who knows how to stand before the Father and pour out His heart and see results—what He prays for is accomplished on earth! There are many unnecessary things to be *unlearned* before we can learn the necessary things. Only then can we understand what Jesus understood and the authority that He had in prayer. We can then develop the passionate heart that He showed for the Father in prayer—and experience the full power of prayer.

Lord, Teach Us

Before we can enter into a season of Holy Spirit-powered prayer, we, like the disciples, need to come to Jesus and say, *"Lord, teach us to pray..."* (Luke 1:1). The prayer that Jesus taught the disciples recorded in Luke 11 is not the prayer that He Himself was praying. Jesus did not pray, *"Forgive us our sins as we forgive those who sinned against us"* because the sinless One had no need for forgiveness. He was not looking for His disciples to learn and memorize His words; instead, He was giving them language to stir their hearts and rouse their passions.

Jesus wanted to give much more than just a few words for them to recite, and the disciples were ready. They knew a little bit about prayer but they were pleading for more. Their plea was, "Jesus, we want a taste of what you have. We want to understand something more than just our basic prayers. We want to understand your heart, Jesus. We want to have an encounter with you as the Divine Intercessor and we want to have your intensity in our prayers. Give us a raging soul for your kingdom. We understand that the Divine Intercessor is in our midst."

Jesus the Intercessor

In order to have a vibrant prayer life, you must understand the function, the authority, and the role of Jesus as the Divine Intercessor. If you do not know or have not encountered the Divine Intercessor yourself, if you have not been with Him, if you are not taking on His Spirit in your life, you will never be able to pray as Jesus prayed. You may be inspired by a sermon and think to yourself, "Oh, God, I am really connected now." You may even covenant to pray, but you will not have the authority or the unction or the spirit to continue fervently in prayer unless you are connected with Jesus Christ.

Hebrews 7:25 describes Jesus as the Divine Intercessor,

Wherefore he is able also to save them to the uttermost that come unto God by him, seeing he ever liveth to make intercession for them (KJV).

He lives to intercede for us! Let me put it in today's terms. He lives for this stuff—this is what He loves to do. In other words, He is saying, "I get my life out of this. This is what gives me energy. This is what gives me joy. This is what I am passionate about. I live to intercede!" And He is still interceding! The Bible says He is now at the right hand of God, interceding day and night on our behalf.

21

The disciples got a glimpse of Jesus as the Divine Intercessor when they saw Him pray and realized that He *lived for prayer*. What was the air that He breathed? It was prayer. He inhaled the presence of God; He exhaled exaltation, intercession, admonition, and encouragement to the Father in heaven. His whole life-flow was prayer.

Hebrews 8 describes how Jesus intercedes. In verse 2 He is described as, *"A minister of the sanctuary, and of the true tabernacle...."* Jesus is serving in a sacred place, the tabernacle. In other words, He is serving and interceding in God's presence, right in the house of God, a house of prayer...*which the Lord pitched, and not man.* You may ask, "What does that mean? Why are you giving us details about the tabernacle set up by God?" If you are ever to have a life of prayer, it is crucial that you understand that Jesus is the Divine Intercessor. You must know that He has set a place for us to pray, for us to seek God, for us to intercede, for us to know Him intimately, and to walk in power and authority. It will revolutionize your prayer life if you understand that He has set up a place, a true tabernacle, that is divinely made. It is not made by man but by the Spirit of the Lord. The Scripture says, "...*Not by might, nor by power but by my Spirit, saith the Lord of hosts" (Zechariah 4:6).*

Jesus is the only way to the true place of intercession. It is not a place that can be found through a formula nor is it a place built "with the hands of man." You can't create this environment on your own. It is a secret meeting place of divine origins, found only in the realm of the Spirit. Jesus has established this place for us and we can now come freely into His presence through His own Spirit.

We need the Spirit of the Divine Intercessor in our lives in order to accomplish anything through prayer. If you are praying but not walking in the revelation of the Divine Intercessor, you are doing what Jesus refers to as "vain repetition." In the book of Matthew, Jesus condemned people who prayed repetitiously. The Pharisees and other religious people prayed certain prayers at certain times of the day and Jesus said it was all done in vain. Now He was not so worried about the repetition—in fact, He encouraged them to pray, to ask, to seek, and to knock. He wants us to keep pressing in more and more. No, He wasn't concerned about the repetition factor—He just knew that it was all in vain. Why was it in vain? Because it was not connected to the Holy Spirit, it was not empowered. It was merely works done by man.

Some people have a religious spirit—a sense of obligation or of duty that makes them feel that they *have* to do things. They have to pray or work by the might of their own power, their flesh. They have certain needs and things they want to see accomplished so they grit their teeth and say, "I'm going to pray until this is accomplished. I am going to see God move." Then they get angry with God because He doesn't seem to be moving. Why isn't He moving? Because they are operating in human power, the power of the flesh. They are ministering in a tabernacle made by the hands of man and not by the Lord. They are not empowered by the Divine Intercessor's love and encouragement in their life.

The Offer of Power

True prayer, true intercession, has to be established by the Lord, as the Scripture says in Hebrews. Jesus Christ Himself must establish it in order for us to connect with the Father. Furthermore, Hebrews 8:3 states,

For every high priest is ordained to offer gifts and sacrifices: wherefore it is of necessity that this man have somewhat also to offer (KJV).

All the high priests in the Old Testament had something to offer. Some would sacrifice, some would sing songs, and others were teachers. Each of the priests had a role.

Yet, as fallen finite creatures, we have nothing to offer the infinite Creator. Here in Hebrews we see that Jesus has something to offer and we need to appropriate it by the spirit of prayer. We need what He has to give to us. We cannot accomplish anything in ourselves. Jesus is offering His life to you. Do you understand this? Do you understand that true prayer is given by the Spirit of the Lord, that He wants to offer you the power to pray?

On several occasions Jesus said something, or prayed something, or asked the Father something out loud. He knew that the Father heard whether it was said audibly or not, but He said it out loud so that those who heard would understand and be drawn into the spirit of prayer that He had. He seemed to constantly be stirring their hearts by offering a revelation of His own prayer life to them. He is the firstfruits of a life we are to inherit. If you are sons or daughters of Jesus Christ, you are

"...partakers of the divine nature [of God]" (2 Peter 1:4). Where is the Spirit that was in Christ Jesus? The Spirit of the Divine Intercessor dwells within every believer who longs to be filled with His power.

The Gift of Desire

What specifically does Jesus offer us? The Holy Spirit says through the Scriptures, *"Let this mind be in you which was also in Christ Jesus" (Philippians 2:5).* Jesus says He offers His mind, His Spirit, His heart, His intercession, and His prayers. He tells us, "The Divine Intercessor in Me will now become the God-led intercessor in you. Your prayers will be of heaven and not of man. They will be exalted prayers, prayers that the Lord will give you."

I love Psalm 37:4:

Delight yourself also in the Lord and he shall give you the <u>desires</u> of your heart.

I used to interpret this verse to mean that if I delight myself in the Lord, He will give me whatever I want: that new car, that new house, whatever it might be. But now I believe that it means if I delight myself in the Lord, He will give me desires that are His. I like to put a period after "give you the desires." I want Him to give me the desires. Not just *my* desires but He will put *His* desires in *my* heart.

The Spirit, the Divine Intercessor, will live and breathe and work in you so you will not have to ask, "Teach me to pray." You will never *know* how to pray, you will never *learn* how to pray and you never will *pray* until you partake of the Spirit of the Divine Intercessor.

Many have been taught to pray according to the acronym ACTS:

- adoration
- confession
- thanksgiving
- supplication

But Jesus does not give us an acronym. He does not seem to care about giving us a program or a diagram. No, He wants to breathe the breath of God on us. He wants us to be in His presence, to share in the divine capacity of God. I want to encourage you today—whether you are three years old or 103 years old, to desperately cry out of your heart to the Father. Jesus is inviting us to become like Him in spirit, whom the Bible says, *lives to intercede (Hebrews 7:25).*

Luke 10:38-42 presents an object lesson through two sisters, Mary and Martha. Mary chose to sit at the feet of Jesus and listen to His words while Martha stayed busy serving. While Martha was occupied by what seemed to be urgent, Mary chose what was important. She chose to learn more of Jesus. In this context Jesus talked to His disciples about prayer. He called His followers to choose what is best, that is, to sit at His feet. Mary learned the power of anointed, godly prayer because she was willing to spend time with Jesus. Mary sat at the feet of Jesus and He said, "She has chosen what is best." Didn't Martha choose what was best? After all, she was serving everyone's needs. We have many Martha's in churches today who think they are choosing what is best because they are busy about many things. They are busy with outreaches, functions, meetings, activities and Sunday school classes but they have not chosen what Jesus says is best—sitting at His feet.

He is Building a House of Prayer

Recently, the Holy Spirit lovingly rebuked me. He showed me that our church is busy but few are sitting at His feet. I believe the Lord is glorified by our spirit of worship, by our efforts to win the lost, and by our ministries to children and youth. But there is one thing we seem to be missing: We have not been a praying church. Prayer has never been emphasized and given highest priority and the Lord has made it clear to me that it is time to change. It is time to make our church a house of prayer, not only individual, devotional prayer in private, but also corporate prayer in the assembled congregation.

I can pray when I'm alone—I love praying all by myself. I love to go for walks and pray; I love to pray in my room; I love to lie on the floor, put on some music, and worship the Lord. However, one thing I do not like is to have someone come into the room when I'm praying. Sometimes it seems like people ruin my prayer meetings. When I pray alone I can pray about anything I want. I can kneel, stand, shout, dance, jump—in fact, you don't want to be around me when I'm praying by myself. But if somebody comes into the room when I'm praying, all of a sudden my arms go down by my side or I put them behind my back. "I'm praying for something here and now *you* have come along. You're praying for something totally different and you want me to join you in praying for it?" That takes a different level of concentration and patience.

You see, I have always been good at the devotional prayer life, but I have never been a good corporate prayer person. At the beginning of this year the Lord spoke, "This church is going to become known as a house of prayer." I asked Him, "Well, Lord, who is going to lead it? Send somebody good to lead the house of prayer and I will support them; I will be in my room praying for them. Oh, Lord, let them have a great time as they are leading and disrupting each other and praying about Aunt Betty's corn on her toe and…whatever. But I will get into the real prayer here with my devotional life."

The Lord is teaching me now, just as He taught me when I could not pray for five minutes. Now I cannot spend less than an hour in prayer. Likewise, He is going to teach us to pray together. If you do not pray alone, if you do not have a devotional prayer life, then you may want to learn how to enjoy prayer with others. God wants us to move into that.

We are created for more than just devotional prayer. The Lord is saying, "Jump into the water. Get together with other people and learn to pray together." If the Lord is going to establish a house of prayer, we are going to have to learn to get together and say, "Yes, Lord" to church prayer meetings. As the Lord establishes a house of prayer we should not *"touch it with the hands of man" (Hebrews 9:11)*. That is, we should not tell God, "This is how we're going to do it. Here is the training we will do. Here are the steps we will take." No, we are to wait on Him until He tells us when and how long we should get together for prayer. We want the Lord to orchestrate and guide us into the way He has for us.

Jesus wants us to learn to pray corporately and also alone. Real, anointed, divine intercessory prayer occurs both when you are praying alone to God and also when the church comes together. Some of you think you are made only for individual private prayer but God says to give your heart also to corporate prayer; you are made for that as well. Unlike any time in the history of the church, our generation is attempting to exist without the church prayer meeting. As a result, we have little true power from on high.

A Parable of Divine Intercession

Connected to teaching the disciples The Lord's Prayer (Luke 11:2-4), Jesus added a core precept of prayer in a parable (Luke 11:5-8). What He seems to be saying is that it is not enough to understand the ingredients of prayer; we must have a burning heart for prayer. He illustrates this through a parable of a person who petitions in utter desperation, then He tells them, "Now, here is the real heart of the matter. If you are ever going to pray these words that I have just told you to pray, if you are ever going to pray anything more than just memorized prayers, you are going to have to understand the parable I am about to teach you. Understanding and applying this precept is necessary if your prayers are to be anything more than memorized words."

Jesus goes on to say, "Suppose one of you goes to a friend at midnight to ask him to lend you three loaves of bread." This is an imposition, an inconvenience, and, to some degree, unreasonable. At midnight, in a dark house, this really is an unreasonable prayer.

The other day I was making a chocolate milkshake—I love them! In fact, I was making enough for two shakes, one for me and one for my middle son, Evan. Evan was excited because Dad was making a milkshake and he was going to share it—that father/son thing together. This is a big thing in our household. Well, I got some of the ingredients out and started making my masterpiece. Let's get the ice cream in there—now pour chocolate sauce on it. Next, the milk. I opened the refrigerator door and discovered to my dismay that there was no milk! Tragedy! What do we do? No milk! I couldn't just have ice cream with chocolate sauce on it—I wanted a milkshake! Evan and I had our hearts *set* on that milkshake. Oh, we could mix it a little bit more, but we still needed milk.

Since it was only about 5:30 in the evening, I thought I'd go to our neighbor and ask for milk. The time of day wasn't a problem, but I quickly realized there were other problems. I started thinking to myself, "You know what? I'm embarrassed to ask to borrow milk. What if my neighbor asks what I want the milk for? Am I going to tell her that I have ice cream with some chocolate sauce on it but no milk to make a milkshake? Why is anybody borrowing two ounces of milk?" I was too embarrassed to do it, so like any good father, I asked my son to go. "Evan, why don't you go over and borrow a cup of milk from the neighbor?" It can be embarrassing for some of us to admit we have a need.

In Jesus' parable, it wasn't dinnertime when the man

knocked at the door; in fact, it was extremely late at night. You know full well that you don't knock on your friend's door at midnight unless it's important. Your friend is asleep and you wouldn't even telephone him that late unless it was an emergency. But you go, anyway, with audacity because you are desperate. And even when you do knock, your friend may not answer unless you are persistent. Jesus is saying here, "I want you to understand that some prayers need to be prayed out of a desperate midnight cry. There is an unreasonable type of praying." Likewise when *you* pray, you need to *pray with audacity*. You need boldness—you need to come with a sense of urgency. Above all, you must be persistent. You need to access the Father's throne room and plead with Him, "Lord, change the world. Lord, your will be done on earth as it is in heaven." We must not give Him rest until He establishes peace (Isaiah 62:6-7). My concern is that the church does not really know how to pray. And until we get on our knees and begin to cry out to God and seek His face, we will never learn to pray.

What was the reason behind this midnight cry? What drove this person to become a desperate seeker? He confesses the reason for his passionate request when he says, "I have nothing." The attitude that we must bring to God in prayer is simply this: *I have nothing*. We must get to the point where we stop trying formulas, gimmicks and schemes to help us pray. We must get down on our faces before God and say, "I don't know how to pray as I should. Too often I am not even interested in prayer. I don't take the time—I make all kinds of excuses. I say I have no time to pray, yet I can sit and watch television for two or three hours a day. To tell you the truth, Lord, I have nothing. I have nothing to bring to you. I have nothing to offer you." This is the heart of the matter. We must confess to the Lord, "We need you because we have nothing in ourselves."

Going Beyond Friendship to Boldness

Notice how often "friend" is repeated in this parable; it is one of the key words in the entire passage.

And he said unto them, Which of you shall have a friend, and shall go unto him at midnight, and say unto him, Friend, lend me three loaves; For a friend of mine in his journey is come to me, and I have nothing to set before him? And he from within shall answer and say, Trouble me not: the door is now shut, and my children are with me in bed; I cannot rise and give thee. I say unto you, Though he will not rise and give him, because he is his friend, yet because of his importunity he will rise and give him as many as he needeth (Luke 11:5-8 KJV).

In verse 8, Jesus says that even though a friend will not answer *just because he is a friend*, he will answer a *bold, urgent request* made without respect to time, if we are persistent.

Many of you say you are a friend of Jesus. You have a devotional Bible and spend time in devotions every day. But this parable is saying you will not receive or understand the power, the intensity, and the authority of the Divine Intercessor unless you understand that you need more than a good devotional life. You cannot just say, "I am a friend of Jesus. I love Jesus." You must have more than just a casual acquaintance with God. You must have an intense cry of the heart. You must, like the Divine Intercessor, "...*live to intercede" (Hebrews 7:25).* Prayer becomes your lifeblood. You become intensely hungry to see God's face and you pray in the Spirit for the power of the Divine Intercessor. This sincere heart attitude does not come to the casual seeker nor to the one who has chosen an easy, convenient, and self-absorbed lifestyle. It does not come just because you are a friend; it comes because of your boldness, urgency, and persistence.

You may not rise from sleep in the middle of the night to think about a friend, but unusual sounds in the night will stir you. In particular, two types of sounds tend to get your attention and awaken you. The first is a sudden loud boom or thud, which evokes curiosity or fear. The second is the steady drip, drip, drip of a leaky faucet, which is annoying or irritating. You try to ignore it, but it will not go away. Finally, you are forced to get up and check all the faucets. Until the dripping is stopped, you cannot go back to sleep.

Just as we are awakened and moved to action by a persistent, repetitious sound, the Lord hears our persistent, bold prayers. Jesus may ask, "What is that? Why do you keep bringing that matter before me? I know you are my friend and I know you are my follower. I know you have a devotional life, but why this repetitious, persistent prayer?"

"Save my son, save my daughter.
God, change my heart, change my heart.

Cleanse my soul, cleanse my soul, cleanse my soul.
Change this city, change this city.
Save the lost, save the lost, save the lost.
Give me boldness to witness, boldness to witness."

Isaiah 63:15 refers to this as zealous striving. It is full of zeal. There is a striving, a passion. The Bible says the Lord hears our prayer because of our boldness. Figuratively, God gets up to "check the dripping faucet." A devotional life alone is good. You may have joy in the presence of the Lord, and blessings and fruitfulness may come out of that. But you have to go beyond that, beyond a friendship-type prayer and into a bold, persistent-type prayer. Do you see the significance of that? The church must become bold. It must come alive! It must seek God's face. It must press on further and say from the heart, "More of you, Lord, more of your life, more of your Spirit, more of your power, more of your holiness, higher praise, higher prayer, higher power. Come, Lord Jesus, come. Teach us to pray. Be our power to pray."

Do you struggle to pray? Perhaps your prayer life is minimal or even nonexistent, or maybe it has ebbs and flows. You have a few good days but most are less than good. You have tried the formulas, the techniques, and the memorization to no avail. But be assured of this, when you get a glimpse of Jesus as the Divine Intercessor, you will begin to see prayer in a different light. You will personally know the authority, power and intensity of the Divine Intercessor as He works in you and through you.

Day and Night
Persistent Prayer

And he spake a parable unto them to this end, that men ought always to pray, and not to faint; Saying, There was in a city a judge, which feared not God, neither regarded man: And there was a widow in that city; and she came unto him, saying, Avenge me of mine adversary. And he would not for a while: but afterward he said within himself, Though I fear not God, nor regard man; Yet because this widow troubleth me, I will avenge her, lest by her continual coming she weary me.

And the Lord said, Hear what the unjust judge saith. And shall not God avenge his own elect, which cry day and night unto him, though he bear long with them? I tell you that he will avenge them speedily. Nevertheless when the Son of man cometh, shall he find faith on the earth? (Luke 18:1-8 KJV)

Through this parable Jesus taught His disciples an important principle of prayer. He did not just tell them about prayer, He showed them, through the impact of this parable, the lifestyle of day and night persistent prayer. He was not just encouraging them, He was not just challenging them, or giving them a three-point sermon on how to pray better. He wanted to show them the power of persistent prayer. He wanted them to grasp firmly the life of prayer that He had taught them—to see in their mind's eye a picture of the constant, determined prayer life that He desired for them to live. He wanted their lives to become like this widow who was persistent in prayer day and night.

Jesus' words are written for our encouragement and edification and are just as real for us today as they were for His disciples. He is not speaking to a few select saints, or a few "Holy Rollers" who are excited about the Lord, but to all who sense the call and hunger for something deeper.

When we attempt to engage in persistent prayer, many of us feel like giving up within the first few minutes. The first half-hour may often seem miserable to you, but Jesus shows us in this parable that there is a reward if we don't give up. There is a blessing that God wants to give to His people. A man or woman of God who is going to become a day and night persistent prayer must learn to go beyond the starting line and press the race to its completion. That is where the reward awaits.

Why was the heart of Jesus so passionate to teach the disciples to pray relentlessly? Isn't that too extreme? Isn't that too radical for our culture today? If you aren't going to get what you are praying for, wouldn't you be wise to stop and do something else? Jesus encourages us not to give up, because we commonly give up too soon. Just when the breakthrough is on the horizon we stop praying. And because we give up, we do not receive God's blessings for our persistent praying.

Why does God call a people to be radically set apart to pray revolutionary continual prayers? Look at the conditions surrounding the widow and her culture and compare them with the conditions in your own life, specifically the conditions of your church, your city, your children, your marriage and your spiritual walk. Jesus says these things are worth the time and energy necessary to go to the Lord in persistent prayer. He says emphatically that some needs cannot be winked at or overlooked. Some needs are so important and so urgent that it takes someone, whether you are a king, a judge, a ruler, a prince, a pauper, or a widow, who will come boldly and persistently before the Lord. The woman in this parable understood that some things are important enough to merit unrelenting pleading or prayer.

Jesus began the parable by stating, *"In a certain town there was a judge who neither feared God nor cared about man."* Judges in Israel at that time were not at all like the judges in our legal system that attempt to radically separate church and state. Those judges were actually religious leaders who made up the spiritual leadership of their nation. They were the elders, deacons, pastors, shepherds, teachers and rulers, and they were supposed to give leadership to the kingdom of God in the midst of the people.

The woman in this parable recognized that something

was very wrong with this judge even though he was a spiritual leader. He had no fear of God and no sense of the need for the Holy Spirit's power to accomplish God's work in his life. He did not sense his helplessness. This judge was not a leader who knew how to humble himself before the mighty presence of God. He was a spiritual leader who thought he was wise and clever and did not need the authority of God in his life. He had an attitude of arrogance.

In a similar way, we sometimes believe that our skill, eloquence, wisdom, musical ability, and leadership can make the church a mighty force without the fear of God. There was a time in my life when eloquence, wisdom, and cleverness were the key words in my agenda to build a church. The Lord lovingly humbled me and broke my heart. He showed me that it is foolish to try to accomplish something in the spiritual realm without the power and guidance of the Holy Spirit. *"Unless the Lord builds the house, they labor in vain who build it" (Psalm 127:1).* The judge in this parable is a man who is laboring in vain.

On the other hand, here is a widow crying on behalf of her own spiritual leadership. I thank the Lord for those who hide themselves in the prayer closet. I know that generations ago, my great-great-grandmother prayed for her family. She was not a spiritual leader; she just hid herself in her prayer closet and prayed that God would give her a family of Christian leaders. Her son became an evangelist; her grandson became a pastor and an administrator of a denomination. Her great-grandson became an evangelist and pastor and her great-great-grandson is writing this book. All in answer to the persistent prayers of a woman very few people have ever heard of. Although many people have heard of David Wilkerson, her great-grandson, very few people have heard of her. She was one of these praying women—a widow in the closet praying for spiritual leadership in the church.

You may believe you fear God, but deep down you think you can handle life on your own, set your own agenda, and take care of your own needs. You think that your knowledge, wisdom, and resources give you the power to do whatever you want. Without a true fear of God, you will not humble yourself before Jesus and admit that nothing in the spiritual realm can be accomplished without His help. If you are not praying from the heart, you do not fear God. Let's look at the parable again. We see that the judge is lost in his rebellion toward God. Amazingly, he recognizes his spiritless, godless leadership. *"I know that I do not fear God. Even though I don't fear God, she continually bothers me."* Here is a man who is so far from God that he has lost the anointing touch that was intended to be on his life for leadership in the community of believers. He is lost, and even though he recognizes it, he still doesn't care. The Bible says this man did not care about his fellow man—he was a leader in name only. All he cared about was himself, his position, his power, and his authority. He was not a *true* spiritual leader.

The widow in this parable was discerning and she recognized that something was wrong in her city and with its spiritual leader.

There was in a city a judge, which feared not God, neither regarded man: And there was a widow in that city; and she came unto him, saying, "Avenge me of mine adversary" (Luke 18:2-3).

She came to the judge with a plea, a desperate cry in her heart, a hunger, a thirst for justice and righteousness. *"Give me justice against my adversary...."* She wanted a wrong to be righted and she may not have known that the unspiritual judge was part of the problem. Spiritual leadership is often the most averse to the true movement of God.

Many times church leaders are at odds with the kingdom of God because they do not walk in the fear of God. They are more concerned about creating personal empires, building bigger churches, increasing membership numbers, and amassing finances than they are about the kingdom of God. I have sat with pastors at conferences and listened as the conversation devolved to a self-serving discussion of the number of attendees they have on Sunday, the size of the weekly offering, and what kind of building program they are pursuing. When I tried to change the subject to Jesus, there was no interest at all. These church leaders, so-called men and women of God, obviously have no real fear of God.

I am not pointing the finger at others—all of us get off track occasionally. But when the Holy Spirit comes to us and we recognize Him, we fall on our faces before God in humility and repentance. We confess to the Lord that we have been wrong and we ask Him to change us and make us spiritual leaders. We do not want to be lost in self-seeking kingdom building. If the Lord is calling you into a place of leadership, whether it is the simplest form or whether it is some place of authority, pray that your heart will be humbled and broken before the Lord.

We need people in the church today who are willing to pray until the windows of heaven are opened and the church experiences fire and zeal. A church touched by the dynamic power of the Holy Spirit will have a heart for the poor and reach out to the lost. They will no longer care just for themselves—how good they look or how their finances are doing. This type of church will know how to fall on its face before the Lord. It might be a church full of widows but it will be a church that prays. It will be a church that walks in righteousness before God.

The widow in this parable understood the meaning of the phrase, "like shepherd, like sheep." She was not just pointing an accusing finger at the spiritual leadership of the church and saying, "How tragic that our leaders have fallen. How sad that they are not preaching righteousness." I believe she understood that God had a covenant with His people to give them shepherds after their own heart. He will give people shepherds who resemble them in heart and passion. As the saying goes, "Birds of a feather flock together." You will be most comfortable under leadership that is like-minded. And, if you are comfortable under that leadership, you will be persuaded to be like the leaders.

Let's look at this widow again. She is crying out, not just for godless leaders who do not have the fear of

God, but also for those who follow these leaders. If the shepherd is corrupt, not fearing God, and not caring for people, what will be the condition of his flock? In Ezekiel 34, we see God's broken heart over shepherds who do not care for people. They only care about their agendas, their structures, their systems, their style, their homes, their prosperity, their wealth, their care, their feeding, and their self-nurture. God says He is going to pull the rug out from under them.

Halfway through that very same chapter, God turns the tables when He asks, "But what about you sheep? What about my flock? It is not just the leadership, it is the flock, as well." He describes how people have trampled on one another, and points out sins abounding in the flock. Some care nothing about others. Some have broken relationships and do not seek restoration. Others are gossips. Some in the flock have not repented of their own sin. They would rather point the finger at others in the flock and in the leadership. They don't look at themselves and say, "God, my heart is broken over my sinful condition. Please forgive me."

The widow in the parable is not in a place of authority or a position of power, but she is humbly seeking God's face. She is not driven by ambition or her own agenda. Then why is she crying out to God like this? Because she is brokenhearted over the condition of the church and the fallen nature of her city.

If this widow were alive today, she would compare the spiritual condition of today's church with the spiritual condition of the churches described in Revelation 3.

She would cry out to God, "Look at the church of Sardis that has lost its first love. Oh, God, that describes our flock. Lord, touch us who have lost our first love." When she read about the lukewarm Laodicean church she would cry, "Oh, God, look at our lukewarm hearts." I can picture her praying day and night, "Lord, I know it is early, but do you see the condition of the church? Do you see the trouble that we are in? Do you see the brokenness of our soul? Do you not see these things, God?" God answers, "Yes, I see them. I hear your heart's cry."

Noontime comes and the widow runs some errands. Then she returns and begins to pray again, "Oh, God, don't you see the broken condition of the church? Our spiritual leadership is crumbling; our hearts are far from you. There is lukewarmness in your church and so many of us do not even care." She is crying out to God about an adversary. She is pleading with tears in her eyes. "Oh, God, there is an adversary. There is the evil enemy, Satan himself. There is the flesh, sin, and the world. These are the adversaries coming against us."

Many of us have no defense against the enemy because we are not seeking God's face. We are not crying out to him day and night, asking him to raise up a standard when the enemy comes in like a flood. Therefore, many are being overwhelmed. God is raising up widows like this in the church who are saying, "Lord, enough of this. Enough of this flood that is destroying your church and causing our cities to be rampant with sin." God is calling all of us to be like this widow, to understand day and night intercession before the Lord. He wants us to be humble servants who lock ourselves in the closet and say, "Lord, we will give you no rest day or night. We want to be your watchmen." This was not something this woman just happened to stumble into. The Bible says that *God sets watchmen* in places who will call on His name day and night.

> *I have set watchmen upon thy walls, O Jerusalem, which shall never hold their peace day nor night: ye that make mention of the Lord, keep not silence, And give him no rest, till he establish, and till he make Jerusalem a praise in the earth (Isaiah 62:6-7 KJV).*

They will give God no rest until He makes the church a place of His praise.

God Comes to the Humble Intercessor

Jesus selected this poor humble woman so that He could show us, through her, how to pray. What was it about her? It was not her skill, eloquence, or cleverness. She had nothing to offer this judge, and that is why he kept putting her off. But she had something that God saw and she received His favor. She had a "day and night persistence" and she continued to come to the judge. She was like the proverbial hound of heaven.

If you do not know how to pray, just keep coming to the Lord. If you do not know the words to say, just keep coming. If you do not seem to have the right heart, just keep coming. If you do not know how to pray anointed prayers, keep praying. Some people stop praying because there are no feelings of anointing. Some of the most effective prayers you will ever pray have no sense of anointing to them at all. You will stop coming if you wait for your prayers to have the feeling they are anointed. Don't depend upon your feelings. If you have a right heart, every prayer you pray will be anointed even though you don't think so. Just keep coming and God will answer you. He will give you a stirring of the soul. He will give you burdens and passions in your heart and you will begin to pray for justice against our adversary. That is what the widow did. She gave the judge no rest day and night. She had an attitude of faith that was unwilling to give up. She chose not to give up until there was a breakthrough. She had faith!

The Prayer of Faith

Jesus asked a probing question at the end of His parable. "When the Son of Man comes back, will there be anybody with faith like this widow?" You see, it is faith that allows you to be persistent in prayer. Why were the other widows in this town not crying out over the wickedness of their city? Because they did not have faith. Either they didn't have the burden or they were apathetic, so they did not pray. But *this* widow was not like that. Persistent people like this widow will be the ones who are willing to give up everything for the kingdom of God and come day and night, crying out to God.

We do not know the specific reason or the particulars of the situation that made her go knocking on the judge's door, but we *do know* that everything was resolved. Because of her persistence, this woman wore down this unrighteous judge and he moved to grant her request.

Now put yourself in the judge's shoes. After he granted the widow's request, he was thankful that he was finally rid of her and he hoped he never had to see her again. However, her successful campaign of persistent pleading only encouraged her to return to plead other causes. Likewise, when we see answers to persistent prayer, our faith is increased and we keep coming to God in prayer. If we are given an inch, we will take a mile. When we begin to learn the effectiveness of prayer, when we pray and God grants us our request, there is a connection with Him. He puts the desire in our hearts, we offer it back to Him in prayer, and then we see the kingdom of heaven open up as our prayers are answered. When we see prayer answered, we go back with more prayer—just like this widow.

I believe the widow hounded that judge for the rest of his life. In fact, he probably wanted to move to a whole different province just to get away from her because he knew that she would not give him any rest until he granted her requests. This is not to say that God resists us or that we are a bother to Him. Far from it! Jesus is just saying through the parable that an ungodly, unrighteous, and unjust judge is bothered by these things, but the living God is righteous, just, and merciful, and He is delighted to have His children come to Him so He can grant them the desires of their heart.

I must tell you honestly, however, that there are seasons when God does *delay* an answer because He wants those who commune with Him to be persistent. God is not a genie in a bottle; He doesn't want casual seekers offering dead prayers expecting their requests to be answered. He wants hungry people whose hearts have been won by Him, people who will seek Him whether they see the answer or not—just because they love Him. Sometimes He will actually delay an answer in order to see if you are willing to be hungry, thirsty, and persistent.

I want to challenge you to get started. Constantly pursue the heart of the Lord and seek His desires for your heart. Are you willing to pray as persistently as Jesus prayed? Are you that hungry? Are you that thirsty?

Going Beyond Prayer

And coming out, He went to the Mount of Olives, as He was accustomed, and His disciples also followed Him. When He came to the place, He said to them, "Pray that you may not enter into temptation." And He was withdrawn from them about a stone's throw, and He knelt down and prayed, saying, "Father, if it is Your will, remove this cup from Me; nevertheless not My will, but Yours, be done." Then an angel appeared to Him from heaven, strengthening Him.

And being in agony, He prayed more earnestly. And His sweat became like great drops of blood falling down to the ground. When He rose up from prayer, and had come to His disciples, He found them sleeping from sorrow. Then He said to them, "Why do you sleep? Rise and pray, lest you enter into temptation" (Luke 22:39-46).

We all know that Jesus gave His life to prayer. Likewise, we can be certain, as His followers, that it is His divine desire to bring each of us into this same passion for prayer.

The event recorded in Luke 22 occurred just before the last day of Jesus' life. He could have been addressing a thousand issues, teaching in vital places, or meeting with the future leaders of the church, but He wasn't. Instead, Jesus was giving His time, passion and energy to prayer. We tend to think prayer is an attachment to our many demands and agendas—but to Jesus prayer *was* His agenda. Nothing drew His heart like communion with the Father and He wanted His disciples to follow His lead.

After celebrating Passover that evening, Judas Iscariot betrayed Jesus. Then Jesus was taken before the Sanhedrin and the counsel—and the very next day He was crucified. Jesus knew that His time was short and He wanted to model prayer one last time to a few of His disciples. He wanted to show them how to pray earnestly, not just casually. He wanted them to know how to really seek the kingdom of God, how to intercede, and how to walk earnestly with Him. He said to them, "A while back you asked Me to teach you to pray and now I'm going to draw you into an even *deeper* place of prayer." For three years Jesus had been on this prayer journey with them, demonstrating how to come to a place of intercession, a place of seeking the Father's face.

Look at Luke 21:37: *"And in the day time he was teaching in the temple...."* This was the last week of His life and He was using His time wisely, daily teaching in the temple. *"...and at night he went out, and abode in the mount that is called the mount of Olives"(KJV)*. Again we find Him praying (22:39), *"Jesus went out as usual to the Mount of Olives..." (LB).*

What was Jesus doing those nights? I believe He was spending entire nights in prayer away from the crowds. It was just a twenty-minute walk up to a beautiful place out of Jerusalem called the Garden of Gethsemane and this was His usual place to pray. You see, He had a *set place* and a *set time* to pray.

Jesus didn't have a "Daytimer" or a computer to record His schedule like most of us do. His internal timetable kept track of when He would be with his Father. There He would pray for His disciples and intercede for those who were not yet born into the kingdom of God. We know that Jesus commonly went to this place to pray "as usual."

Time to Follow

The disciplined person has "usual" prayer, prayers that are prayed often as a routine part of life. Time set aside for dynamic, consistent prayer is vital to spiritual growth. Jesus had this discipline in His life and He invited His disciples to do the same. *"...and his disciples followed him"* (verse 39). Are you a disciple of Jesus Christ? Are you following Him into a life of prayer? Have you heard His invitation, His wooing? Make Jesus your role model in prayer!

Jesus sits at the right hand of God and *"...He is always living to make petition to God and intercede with Him..."(Hebrews 7:25 Amp.).* Isaiah 56:7 says, *"There's joy for him in the house of prayer."*

Let me ask you some personal questions:

- Are you following Jesus into the house of prayer?
- Are you following Him into a "usual" place where you pray?
- Do you pray regularly?
- Do you pray daily for your spouse and your children? Do you intercede on their behalf? Jesus says to his disciples, *"Pray that you don't fall into temptation"(Luke 22:46).*

Fathers, you need to pray for your children that they don't fall into temptation. The world has a lot to offer them. You need to be praying that your children will be raised up as mighty men and women of God as they grow.

Wives, do you pray for your husbands? Do you pray that God's hand will be upon him? Do you pray that God will fall upon him with power and might and truth in his life?

Single person, do you take some of the time that you have in your busy days and schedule to literally set apart a "usual" time of day when you cry out to God? It doesn't matter if it is morning, afternoon or evening, you need to be meeting regularly with God, praying, "Jesus, give me more of your heart. Give me more of your life. Let me be like you."

Children, young people, teenagers, are you seeking the Lord's face? The Old Testament says to set your face *"like a flint toward God" (Isaiah 50:7)* so that you won't be swayed by the temptations of the world. You need to begin this early in life.

Jesus' own life was a model of what He wanted to see established in His disciples (and that means us, because we are His disciples). If we are honest with ourselves, many of us have to admit that we don't have "usual" times of prayer. Sometimes we may go days without a consistent time and place of prayer where we can openly and transparently commune with God away from the distractions of the world.

Many of us mistake the practice of frequent "prayers of the moment" for a disciplined commitment to prayer. What I mean by that is "as you go" type of prayers. I pray those all the time and I encourage you to do this, as well, whenever you have time to spend a few minutes in prayer.

For example, I live a considerable distance from our church building and I sometimes use my commuting time to listen to a cassette tape of a sermon, or inspiring music. I often find myself praying or worshiping Him. At other times, I pray while performing some routine task, such as walking down the aisles at the grocery store. I'm sure those prayers glorify the Lord and it is a time to connect with Him, but that can't be your life source for intimacy with Jesus. This won't result in your being consumed with the Father's house. It just won't happen in an "as you go" manner.

Husbands, what if you told your wife today, "I really love you, honey, and enjoy being with you, but you know I'm a very busy man. We can spend time together but it has to be while I'm doing something else. I can't set aside time just for you. You can ride to work with me and then take the bus home. I have to go to the grocery store tonight and I'll let you accompany me. I need to mow the lawn on Saturday morning and I'll be up bright and early, so you can walk along with me. I'll try to keep the noise from the mower down so I can hear you when you shout things into my ear." Do you think your wife would be happy with you? Absolutely not! You see, she needs time that is not on a casual, "as you go" basis.

In a parallel way, can you imagine how the Lord feels when you give Him just tokens of your time—at your convenience? Tragically, sometimes we don't even give Him that. We give more attention to the sports news or current events report on the radio than we do to Him. It is so easy to allow the world to claim all your time.

The lover of your soul covets time alone with you. The Bible says that God is a jealous God. He is jealous for your time, your love, your affection, your intimacy, and your zeal. He wants you to be consumed with His house. He wants you to care enough about the people around you to lift them up in prayer. He wants you to praise and exalt Him—day in and day out. As the Bible says in Isaiah 62:7, pray *"...till he makes Jerusalem* (your church assembly) *a praise in the earth."* Give God no rest!

Praying like this is a far cry from a casual prayer squeezed into a hurried schedule. Jesus desires much more than leftovers; He cherishes His exclusive time. *"You are my beloved and I am yours. Come away with me,"* he said in the Song of Solomon.

Scheduling is crucial; unless you schedule significant times to be alone with God, the business of life will surely keep you from meeting with Him. You will not have a "usual" time to be with God unless you make it your highest priority.

God doesn't care what time of day you meet with Him—after all, He's available all the time, "24/7" as we say today. Once you schedule your time, don't let anything come between you and Him. Make this time a priority because it will be the most important time in your life. Determine beforehand not to let the tyranny of the urgent take the place of what is important.

I schedule one day a week when I am not going to let anything interrupt my time with the Lord. I am learning to honor my commitment to God and say "no" to everything else.

The Place of Prayer

It was usual for Jesus to pray, and He invites us to have a consistent, daily time of prayer. We read in verse 40, *"When He came to the place…"* It's not only vital to have a scheduled *time* of prayer, it's important to have a *place* of prayer. As you attempt to incorporate more prayer into your life, you may notice that certain places are more conducive to praying than others. For instance, the football stadium during a game is not the most favorable place to pray—unless you're praying, "Oh, God, please help our team win."

Jesus had a usual *time and place* where He met with the Father—the garden on a hill outside the city of Jerusalem. He selected the most beautiful place, the quietest place that He knew.

Have you ever scheduled a meeting with someone

and not included a place to meet? If I were to say to you, "Hey, I have really been looking forward to getting with you. Can we meet at lunch tomorrow about noon? Great! See you then." Would that be complete? No, obviously not. An appointment must include a *time and a meeting place*. Don't rob yourself of a real prayer time because you don't expend the energy to create a regular place to pray. Your place of prayer can be anywhere that suits you, be it a park or a quiet room. It can be anywhere that is right for you.

Don't let the children bother you. You get a babysitter so you can go to a movie, so why not get a babysitter so you can be alone with God? God is saying, "Find a place, find a time, and find a season. Have a heart to get alone with Me."

A Heart for God

You will never do anything about prayer if you don't have a heart for God. That must be your starting place. Talk to God, "Father, I probably would not have been one of those disciples who followed you into the garden. I probably would have been too busy with my job, my family, my social life, or even with programs at church." Admitting to yourself that you are not praying "usual" prayers might be the beginning of introducing your heart and your life fully to a place of prayer.

A parallel passage, Mark 14: 33, tells us that Jesus *took* Peter, James and John and *drew* them away into the garden with Him. As I was reading this I prayed, "Lord, that's what I want in my life." And I can assure you that this is what I pray for my church, "Oh, God, take us into the garden. Don't just suggest it to us—don't just try to encourage us. No, Lord, we want you to grab hold of us. Grab hold of our hearts and *take* us into the place of prayer." The deepest cry of my soul is, "Take me to you, Jesus. Draw me to you! Lord Jesus, take my heart—my soul—my energy—my time—my schedule— my all! Take me to a place where you want me to be. Take everything that I have, Lord, and let me be centered, rooted, grounded in the house of prayer."

I want Jesus to take my life. When I pray for my church, I cry to Jesus to take hold of every person's heart. "Take it, grab it, snatch it. Crash into each life and say, 'I'm not going to leave you alone.'"

"...I will never leave you nor forsake you" (Hebrews 13:5). We usually think that that passage is sweet and tender. We may think, "Oh, thank you, Jesus. That's so nice." Why would we think that? Because when we don't want to be alone, we are comforted knowing that Jesus is there, tagging alongside. But maybe Jesus was speaking in a totally different way, a way we have never even considered.

"I'm never leaving you! You're going to try to run from Me. In fact, you're going to try to hide, escape, neglect and ignore Me but I will never leave you. I'm going to pursue you. I'm going to chase you and when I get you, I'm going to take you into My hands and give you the fullness that you desire. The hunger of your heart will be met as I take hold of your life."

Jesus took Peter, James and John into this wonderful

place. I believe Jesus wants the cry of our hearts to be, "Lord, take me to greater depths of prayer and places of intercession than I've never known before. Take me to revelations of the Father's heart that I've never begun to glimpse or even imagine. Father, take me into places of intercession for others where my heart begins to pound. Let tears flow as I seek your face like I've never sought you before."

Right now some of you are thinking, "Why get so passionate about prayer?" Some are already getting disturbed because you don't want to be taken into this place of prayer. You are not comfortable there, and you certainly don't want Jesus to grab you by the scruff of your neck and say, "You must come into My presence. You must have time alone with Me."

Why don't we want to be taken into this place? Let me share two reasons:

1. FEAR

First, we often neglect or actively run from the call to the prayer closet (the house of prayer) because we've experienced a taste of what it is to get into that place, and the intimacy with God scares us.

As I was praying recently, I asked the Lord, "Why is it that sometimes the church seems to be the most ignorant and neglectful of you?" I sensed Him say to me, "People are afraid to come into My presence because if they know My heart intimately, it will break their heart." If we get close to God and He begins to share even a portion of His heart, we become overwhelmed. We may begin to cry when we see that God's heart is so loving and yet so broken over the sin of the world. His heart is broken over the downfallen lukewarm state of the church and the backslidden hearts. His heart is so huge and yet so shattered!

At a recent meeting I was sharing some of the things the Lord has been speaking to my heart about prayer. I felt embarrassed because I began to weep. Like most men, I hate to cry in public, but my heart was deeply wounded over the condition of a church that is so luke-warm. Too many of us are caught in habitual practices of sin that should have been long gone in our lives. As God reveals His heart to us, our own hearts become wounded.

Luke 22:42 shows us the words of Jesus as He cries out, "*...take this cup from me.*" The Word goes on to say, "*And being in anguish...His sweat was like drops of blood falling to the ground*" (*vs. 44*). Now *those* are words of hardship. Our society is averse to hardship and we will do almost anything to avoid it. The burden of the Lord is an offense to us because we prefer to live in pleasure, joy and self-seeking in order to avoid inner conflict of the soul. We want God to tell us that all we have to do is name something and claim it and then feel good about it. In other words, whatever you want, you get. But God wants to give us more than we *want*; He wants to give us what we *need*. God is saying that when we come into His secret place, we may get a broken and a contrite heart—but we will also get a heart that is near to God.

The Scriptures state that it is those with the broken

and contrite hearts, those who have a heart after God, who see His face. They are the ones who have the revelation of what it is to truly know God.

So one obstacle to entering in closer to God is fear— fear that to do so might change us in a radical, dynamic way that would force us outside our comfort zone and cause us some hardship.

2. UNBELIEF

Second, we are reluctant to enter into the house of prayer because of unbelief. What a tragedy! Many in the church are trapped in such strong unbelief that prayer is just a religious structure for them. It has become a religious duty and has nothing to do with the life-flow of their experience because they do not believe that God really answers prayer.

We sometimes see this attitude in our children. When we as parents invite our children into prayer, it hurts to hear them say, "You know, Dad, I don't want to pray."

"Why not, Son?"

"Because I prayed about that already and God didn't do anything about it."

What do you say to children about unanswered prayers? What do you say *to adults* about unanswered prayer? Does it rob our hearts of the belief that God is good? Do we let it rob our hearts of belief in all spiritual matters? Too often the answer is that it does. The result is that our hearts are robbed of faith and we walk around in unbelief. Therefore, why pray if we don't believe God is going to hear us? Why pray if we don't believe God's hand moves on behalf of those who earnestly seek His face? If that's the case, why spend time alone with Him? We might as well do other things because prayer appears to be a waste of time.

Satan has robbed many believers through subtle deception. He convinces them that prayer doesn't work, that it's a waste of time. I doubt that any follower of Christ would stand in a church assembly and actually state, "I am absolutely convinced that prayer is a waste of time and I won't spend time praying because I don't believe God even hears me." You probably wouldn't say it but many of you have that suspicion in your heart. That is the subtle sin of unbelief—and it quenches the Holy Spirit. The Bible says Jesus could do very little in certain places among certain people. Why? Because of their unbelief!

What can be done about a fearful or unbelieving heart? The answer lies in getting to know intimately the heart of God and more clearly understand His love for us. This will require endurance and a willingness to do the work assigned to us. Jesus did not say, "This is too hard, Father—I give up. I don't think you're answering My prayer, anyway." No, He said, "Your will be done, not Mine. If you choose not to answer My prayer in the affirmative, I don't care; I'm still going to be here every night. Every night, Father, I'm here in this *usual* place, to seek your face, to know you so I can know your will. Then I can know your heart and if you say no to my prayer, I will *believe* and not worry. Unbelief cannot enter in."

Do you understand that? Many of us don't spend

the time in prayer necessary to really know God's heart. It takes time to know God's character, His nature, to the point that we can hear Him say *no* to us and still know that He answered our prayer. It may be hard to hear no, because too often we're like spoiled children, finding it hard to accept a denial of our wishes. We have learned all kinds of systems of manipulation: We whine or moan and groan to try to get our way. But God is firm—He will not be moved. We need to know Him well enough to know that whether He is giving to us or withholding from us, it is for our good. We need to *know* Him so we will *trust* Him!

Dry Times

Jesus longs for people who know what it's like to come into this place of prayer—who come even in difficult times, even in dry, desert, wilderness times. Have you ever had dry times in prayer? Perhaps a better question would be, who hasn't? At one time or another we have all seen prayer as a difficult thing. I have even experienced this during times when the Lord was stirring my heart to seek Him more consistently, more earnestly, and more fervently.

When I choose to get into my prayer closet at a set time to be alone with the Lord, an excitement comes to my spirit and I can't wait to get there. Sometimes on my planned day alone with Him I get up excited and think, "Oh, this is going to be so great. A whole day alone with God." It seems that without trying I have the greatest time of prayer. I get on my knees and tell God how wonderful, precious, and powerful He is. I thank Him for divine interventions and tears come as I seek His face. God meets me and I feel His presence in strong ways.

But other mornings I get up thinking, "Lord, I don't want to do this." Maybe I don't say it to Him quite like that, but I say it to myself. I get easily distracted and I just don't feel like praying. As a matter of fact, even if I force myself to start praying I get an overwhelming sense that God is not present. It seems there is a concrete wall between heaven and me. Some people call it a brass heaven—prayers go up but it feels like they bounce right back and land on your shoulders and weight you down. You wonder, what happened to God? Where did He go? Have you ever felt like that?

Jesus Takes us *Beyond*

In Luke 22 we see what happens to the disciples. Jesus invites them into a place of prayer but then verse 41 tells us that He withdrew just a short distance, about a stone's throw beyond where they were. This verse has been such a blessing to me because sometimes I have sensed that the Lord has distanced Himself or withdrawn Himself from me and then I haven't wanted to pray anymore. I have become angry and cranky and said, "God, you're not here anymore. I thought you called me into a life of prayer, but now you're abandoning me." I perceived it as a negative thing until I came into an understanding of this verse. My heart was comforted as I was shown that He didn't withdraw from the disciples to neglect and abandon them because He didn't want their company. Notice it doesn't say He hid in a cave where they couldn't see Him. No, He was just a stone's throw beyond them.

This is an important point! Jesus wasn't ignoring the disciples or trying to get out of their presence. Rather, *He was trying to draw them into a higher place*, nearer to the heart of God. This is the significance of the word *beyond*. "He went a stone's throw *beyond* them." Likewise when Jesus seems *beyond* us, He has not abandoned us; instead, He is calling us to go with Him *beyond* our present prayer boundaries.

Don't you want to be praying beyond what you are praying right now? Don't you want to learn to go to greater heights in prayer? Don't you want to learn to intercede for people and see miracles take place? Don't you want to know the joy of what it's like to explode in celebration over having been on your knees before God and then seeing your prayers answered?

Not long ago my brother-in-law called to let me know that his eleven-year-old daughter was diagnosed with a very severe and advanced case of brain cancer. Radical surgery was performed immediately and after the surgery, her neck was stiff. This was not good and the doctors thought the cancer might have advanced down her spinal cord, potentially resulting in paralysis. They took another test and as my brother-in-law sat in the doctor's office waiting for the results, he wondered, "Are our prayers really going to work on our daughter's behalf?" Actually, he was quite nervous as he sat there.

When the doctor came in, he reported, "It's just some stiffness as a result of tension from the surgery. She has no trace of cancer in her body, no trace of the tumor, nothing in her spine. She has a clean bill of health." According to my sister, my brother-in-law jumped up out of his seat, raised his hands to heaven, and exclaimed, "Yes, God! Yes, God! Yes, God! Oh, sorry, Doctor."

When your prayers are answered like that, when your desperate cries are answered, you lose all sense of propriety and etiquette. You lose all sense of thinking of yourself and what you say. But unless you enter into that time of deep, desperate prayer, you will never have great rejoicing in your life. Unless you're asking God for big, amazing, miraculous things through intercession, you will never know what it's like to praise God with your whole heart. You may sit in church and ask yourself, "Why do we sing so many songs? Why does the worship leader ask us to praise God out loud and say things like 'hallelujah' or 'glory to God'? Why are these people so radical?" Once you have *great* things to be thankful for, because you have asked for *great* things from God, you will have the ability to praise Him for *great* things in your life. You will realize that Jesus has taken you beyond anything you've ever imagined.

When Jesus withdraws *beyond* you, it's not a time to say, "Oh, well, that was nice while it lasted. I had a few good days with prayer and things seemed to go pretty well for a while. I'll get back to it another time." No, the time you sense that the Lord has withdrawn and His presence seemingly is not as strong as before, you need to press on even more. That becomes a time of growth for you, and your intercession will increase. Your prayer life will reach new ground, new height, and new depth. So don't just pray when you feel good, when you feel like praying, when you have a little bit of extra time to pray. Pray when it is hardest to pray; that is when your prayer life will grow explosively. That is when you will find real maturity in your prayer life and you will become a prayer warrior, an intercessor, and a saint who truly knows the heart of God. Jesus longs to raise up people who are willing to pray—no matter what.

Do you want to experience this *beyond* type of prayer—beyond common prayer? Please don't misunderstand me; usual prayers of thanksgiving (for instance, praying over meals), and regular church prayers are good. But do you want to pray beyond that—to get to a height of prayer that you've never experienced before? Many start toward that goal but never attain it. When Jesus withdraws and invites us into a higher place, instead of pressing on we say, "This is too hard," and give up. The Bible helps us understand that when that withdrawing occurs, when that sense of Jesus calling us to a higher place occurs, oftentimes our heart's response is like that of the disciples, "Oh, well, might as well go to sleep." We give in to a spirit of slumber and experience a lessening of energy and a lack of aggressiveness.

Jesus modeled for us the exact opposite response. The Bible tells us that when He was troubled in soul, feeling the greatest anguish any human had ever felt, He prayed *more earnestly*. The result? He was strengthened by an angel straight from heaven!

And there appeared an angel unto him from heaven,
strengthening him (Luke 22:43).

Jesus, encouraged and strengthened in soul, sought
the Father. Instead of asking that His cup of destiny pass
from Him, He prayed with resolve, "Not my will, but
thine be done."

Sleeping Watchmen

Sadly, like many of us, the disciples did not pray
more earnestly when their souls were sorrowful in anguish. What did they do? The Bible says they fell asleep.
They got sleepier and sleepier because of the sadness of
their hearts. Luke 22:45 says, "...*he found them sleep-*
ing for sorrow." They were exhausted and depressed,
and instead of taking it to the Lord and earnestly pressing on, they said, "This is too hard; it's too demanding.
He has gone a stone's throw away, so let Him go on. We
don't want to chase Him around anymore. We don't want
to go beyond where we are. We have given Him three
years of our lives and we've done it all. We've fasted
and prayed and done everything He told us to do and
now He *wants more.* He leaves us here and then expects
us to carry on without Him. Well, this is just too hard
tonight. It's too sorrowful—let's go to sleep."

In the Old Testament the Bible mentions the word
watchmen. In Old Testament times watchmen were paid
to pray full-time; that was their job. Like a priest or a
judge, that was their profession. They were to seek the
face of the Lord on behalf of Jerusalem. However, we
see in Isaiah 56:10 that the watchmen on the wall would

rather sleep than pray. They had an insatiable desire for sleep. Now isn't that amazing? Even the people who were called to be watchmen (and were being paid for it!) loved sleep more than they loved prayer. In the next chapter (Isaiah 57:2), you can almost hear God saying, "You will have plenty of time for sleep after death. Watchmen, wake up! You can sleep later, but right now it is time to wake up. Now is the time to intercede. *Right now* is the time to move. Let the hand of God move in your life."

The first time the disciples asked Jesus to teach them to pray, He told them to say, "Lead us not into temptation." Three other times Jesus taught His disciples to pray and every time He told them, "Pray that you don't enter into temptation because the spirit is very willing." What temptation is Jesus referring to? I suspect that at one time or another all followers of Jesus have had willing spirits. When that happens, your heart says, "Yes, oh yes, God, I want to go *beyond* in prayer. Yes, God, I crave, I hunger, I desire what you have for me." *Your spirit is willing* but your flesh is weak. Jesus says to pray that you don't enter into the temptation of weak flesh. Pray for supernatural strength so that you are not fooled by the fleshly desires for sleep and rest. Pray that sloth and lack of resolve do not keep you from pressing on to higher ground.

Jesus is saying that once you have resolved in your heart to intercede and have set aside your time and a place to meet, pray, "Oh, God, let me not be led into temptation. I will be tempted to say you're not here. I will be tempted to say this is just a waste of time. I will be tempted to say nothing will happen as a result of this. I will be tempted to say I've given enough time. Five minutes, that's long enough. I feel good." Jesus is calling us to persevere, to get beyond the flesh that loves to sleep, our selfish flesh that is easily distracted.

If you persevere and allow the flesh to be diminished, the spirit that is willing will be raised up in your heart. Then you will find prayer, worship and time alone with God to be the highest delight of your life. The greatest joy of your life will be the times you spend alone with God.

Jesus is saying to the church today, "Enough! Enough of churchianity. Get up! Arise! The hour has come." It is time! God is raising up the house of prayer. Will you accept the invitation and enter in? "The hour has come!"

Remnant Intercessors

Gather yourselves together, yea, gather together, O nation not desired; Before the decree bring forth, before the day pass as the chaff, before the fierce anger of the Lord come upon you, before the day of the Lord's anger come upon you. Seek ye the Lord, all ye meek of the earth, which have wrought his judgment; seek righteousness, seek meekness: it may be ye shall be hid in the day of the Lord's anger (Zephaniah 2:1-3 KJV).

We are living in the last days and the Holy Spirit is calling forth what I call "remnant intercessors." These are people who cling to the Lord in the midst of dark and terrifying times, people who covenant with the Lord and exclusively set their faces toward Jesus and Him alone. In every generation the Lord has established a band of brothers and sisters whose sole desire is to seek Him in a world that has abandoned Him.

The time of the Minor Prophets was a period of spiritual catastrophe for the people of Israel, and the book of

Zephaniah is set when there were terrible tragedies and national disasters in the nation. The people had lost sight of the true and living God and had mixed foreign idols in with their worship of Him. When some of their kings became critically ill, they went to the prophets of Baal to seek healing instead of calling on Yahweh or His prophets. Clearly they did not put their hope and trust in the God of their fathers Abraham, Isaac and Jacob.

God's chosen people lost their heart for Him and did not keep Him preeminent in their lives. In His place, they chose all kinds of idolatry. Because of this, God had to get them to a place where they would listen to the message of impending judgment upon the nation. He accomplished this through the proclamations of Zephaniah and the other Minor Prophets.

In 566 B.C. Zephaniah began to proclaim that Jerusalem would be totally destroyed. Its walls would be torn down and the temple shattered and ruined. He declared that Jerusalem would become a place with no life, no vitality, and no spirit of God living through His people.

Twenty years later, in 546 B.C., a dreadful time of devastation fell upon Jerusalem. God had sent initial warnings and judgments; in fact, their enemies came against them and began to take portions of their land. At the time Zephaniah was writing, much of the northern territory of Israel had already been demolished and overrun. This should have been a clear wake-up call to let them know that something was happening. God was trying to get their attention and stir their hearts—and yet they paid no attention to His initial warnings.

Time after time God's prophets warned His children of impending judgment, but they refused to heed the admonitions. The judgment for ignoring the first warning was comparatively small; however, the judgment for each successive ignored warning was more intense and more painful. God kept increasing the severity and frequency of His judgments until His people began to listen.

Zephaniah spoke during the reign of King Josiah, a righteous king who tried to restore a sense of worship and holiness in the nation of Israel. Even though external changes were put in place, the hearts of the people remained the same. Wickedness, violence, and idolatry were rampant in the land in spite of some outward restoration. God was telling the nation through Zephaniah that it was not enough to have mere superficial change and even a king whose heart was right with Him. He commanded the *nation to repent and to return to Him with all their hearts.* Zephaniah describes the consequences of ignoring His warning.

I will utterly consume all things from off the land, saith the Lord. I will consume man and beast; I will consume the fowls of the heaven, and the fishes of the sea, and the stumblingblocks with the wicked; and I will cut off man from off the land, saith the Lord (Zephaniah 1:2-3 KJV).

We see here that God gave a strong warning that judgment was coming upon the nation of Israel. I believe with all my heart that these things were not written just for Zephaniah's day but are for us today as well. God is speaking to His church and we need to take heed! As in

Zephaniah's time, the severity and frequency of each successive judgment increases each time a warning is ignored.

I believe we may have begun to see the first steps of judgment on America, and it is only the beginning. I want to be very clear that I believe we have not seen the full extent of God's judgment yet. We are only beginning to see God's stirring hand, the fire of His zeal, and His consuming jealousy to bring His people back to Him. If we do not take heed and begin to pray and intercede—if we do not get our hearts right with God and repent and call upon His name—we will find that the events of 2001 are just the start of our woes. More cataclysmic events are yet to come. He will increase the intensity and frequency of judgments until His people finally wake up and respond to His call.

Where Judgment Begins

Zephaniah was a brokenhearted prophet because the Israelites would not listen to him. .

I will also stretch out mine hand upon Judah, and upon all the inhabitants of Jerusalem; and I will cut off the remnant of Baal from this place...(Zephaniah 1:4 KJV).

God is saying here that His judgment comes to the nation of Israel *first*. These are powerful words! He does not say that judgment comes over the whole world; He starts off by judging the nation where His people dwell, the place where He has a holy remnant. He does not say that He will shake the whole world, at least not until His people return to Him. The Bible says that judgment begins in the house of the Lord. God's first place of stirring, shaking, and bringing judgments is the church. That is the meaning of the end of verse 4, *"...I will cut off the remnant of Baal from this place."* He does not initially judge the world at large. He did not cut off every trace of Baal from Babylon or every trace of Baal from Assyria, but every trace of Baal *from His people.* Babylonian idolatry did not belong in Israel. He said, "My people should not be doing those things."

Clearly judgment begins in "this place"—the house of the Lord, with His people, the church. The foreign cultures, foreign idols, foreign worship, and worldliness of this culture do not belong in the heart of a believer. The Lord wants to remove every trace of those things from "this place"—His church—because He loves us, not because He hates us. The book of Hebrews says, "Those He loves, He disciplines." The Word clearly states that discipline is not a pleasant thing to endure, yet it is applied to achieve a purpose higher than we could ever know or imagine.

The Lord desires to build His bride, the church, "without spot or wrinkle." He will do whatever it takes to remove every trace of idolatry from "this place"—the church. He will remove whatever idols are visible. God says He will cut out every trace, as well as the dust that was on the idol that fell onto the floor as it was removed. God does not just get rid of the idol but even the remnants and residue of it. *God's work is deep and thorough.*

I have met people who have been set free from

addictions and other major problems in their life. There are heroin addicts who no longer use drugs but still smoke tobacco even though God told them to quit. In His eyes the tobacco is just as big a problem as heroin, because it represents disobedience. Your sin may not be big in your eyes or your family's eyes and the effect on your body may not be as devastating, but in God's eyes it is just as big because He told you to change. He wants to get rid of the big things, but also all the residue of disobedience in your life. Anything that is not like Him does not belong in your life. God wants to get rid of it all; He wants every trace of it cut out.

People who have been involved in various forms of obvious, deliberate sin in the past may think they are much better because they no longer commit that sin. And they may be "better" but they may be compromising in a less obvious way. You see, all sorts of little things are left in our hearts. The Bible says that judgment comes not just because we are grossly wicked and vile, but often because of the trace, the residue, and the "small" things that are still left in us. God has no choice but to bring discipline in our lives, because when God says holy, *He means holy—not partially holy.* His standard is perfection and His call is for us to be holy as He is holy. Therefore, He will remove sin even if He has to use discipline. God's goal is to bring forth purity in us, and holiness that comes from Him alone. When God says through Zephaniah that He "will cut off the remnant of Baal," He means every trace—all the small things!

Coming to the Altar

King Josiah was a young man filled with zeal for the Lord. His passion for righteousness caused him to go all the way for God. This passion, a heart that desires God and nothing else, is needed in every generation. Because of his fervor for God, Josiah went into the temple and destroyed or removed all that was idolatrous. In the process he found a copy of the Law and read from it to the people. As a result, he and all the people *"...made a covenant before the Lord, to walk after the Lord, and to keep his commandments and his testimonies and his statutes with all their heart and all their soul..." (2 Kings 23:3 KJV).* Josiah also broke down the idolatrous "high places" (2 Kings 23:8). The "high places" were places of worship of false gods. They were palaces and the worship consisted of overeating, drunkenness and sexual orgies. Josiah and his army destroyed the high places and ended all worship of idols, and the priests went along with the plan. They further agreed that there would be no more Babylonian idols and no more temples to Baal. But then they sat down in complacency, as we see in verse 9: *"...[they] did not come up to the altar of the Lord."*

True, things were different on the outside. The people were no longer bowing down to Baal but they were not bowing down to God, either. They had not allowed God to do a thorough work in their lives or a deep work in their hearts. When God gave an altar call they refused to come. How tragic it is when spiritual leaders perform all the outward works of ministry and yet are unwilling to bow before the Lord, because they will not give up the lusts of their hearts.

This situation might be compared to a person in modern times who comes to church. He gets rid of the blatant things and makes external changes, but he does not bow to the Lord in his heart and make a complete surrender.

God is looking for remnant intercessors to cry out for the altar to be filled with humble people—those who will say from a broken heart, "I am hungry for more of Jesus! I long for Him to stir my heart." God wants people who don't just make their lives look good outwardly by doing and saying the right things, but who also want their hearts to be changed. These are people who want holiness in the deepest recesses of their life—they want all worldliness and every trace of Baal cut out, and even the dust from their sin to be swept away.

In Search of Holiness

God is searching for people who desire to be *thoroughly* holy. Zephaniah 1:12 states, *"...that I will search Jerusalem with lamps...."* This means He comes, as it were, with lamps looking in the corners, checking the basement areas and places one doesn't routinely go into. He searches our hearts, looking deep, probing stubborn and unknown sins—sins not touched and not repented for. When God brings in His lamps, He introduces us to things we didn't even recognize. His searchlight helps Him find and cut out even the "dust" of our sin so that nothing is left untouched. You may think your life is clean and you should be thankful that God has done a wonderful work. You know that God is graciously working in that area—but what you may not realize is that as soon as He is finished in that area He will lead you into another area. When you feel Him turn His lamp on you, you know there is more to do. God is thorough and will do a powerful work in our lives; He won't stop until everything that doesn't belong is cut out.

Josiah destroyed not only idols but the traces, patterns, and things that reminded the people of the idols, "...*I will cut off the remnant of Baal from this place, and the name of the Chemarims with the priests...*"*(Zephaniah 1:4).* When God brings judgment to the house of the Lord, He includes *all the priests.* These priests were not just slightly in error in their theology, they were pagans. They served false gods and had no mind or heart for the true and living God. They were interested only in their own agenda and glory, and were not devoted to the name of the Lord in any way. They even brought the strange worship of the Chemarims (foreign idols) into the house of the Lord.

God tells us He will cut off this wrong spirit in the priests or, in New Testament terms, the pastors. God says, "I want pastors who are holy devoted to Me, not those who are after superficial or external signs of spirituality." God desires humble leaders who acknowledge the sovereignty of the Lord and serve Him alone. These pastors realize that it is all about Jesus and not about church culture. This is the spirit that was in John the Baptist when he said, "*I must decrease as He increases.*"

Unfortunately, there are too many pastors who say, "I must increase so that Jesus can increase *with me*."

Let's go on to Zephaniah 1:5 where the subject changes to the people, *"And them that worship the host of heaven upon the housetops...."* This verse says that the people worshiped the host of heaven, which sounds pretty good until you understand that "the host of heaven" really means "the armies of God." *They were not worshiping the Lord of hosts; they were worshiping the hosts of the Lord.* In other words, they were worshiping people, angels, power, and authority. They were choosing places of worship on the basis of popularity, notoriety, or celebrity. A similar situation occurs today when people go to church to hear their favorite pastor speak but stay home when another pastor speaks. When you do that you are worshiping "the host of heaven" in a sense. The Lord of hosts says that He will deal strongly with the hearts of those who worship the *hosts*.

Many today worship the hosts of heaven. We idolize churches, movements and even church rituals in various denominations. New methods of doing things captivate people and they end up making idols of the leaders. Then there's worship—and the style of worship. People get hung up on the *style of worship* rather than the *substance of worship* and the heart of the worshiper. I know of people who have left a church because they didn't like the style of worship. That means that instead of worshiping the Lord, they were *worshiping the worship*.

Zephaniah goes on to address another form of improper worship: *"...and them that worship and that swear by the Lord, and that swear by Malcham"(vs. 5).* These were worshipers who worshiped and adored the Lord and even claimed Him as their all-in-all. However, they also swore by Malcham, a false god from Babylon; hence, their worship had a mixed allegiance. Similarly, many today have mixed worship. They worship the Lord while they are also devoted to sports, money, the desires of their heart, and their agendas.

Another form of "mixed worship" is going to church and worshiping God on Sunday morning, then forgetting about Him the rest of the week. God wants us to worship Him continuously, not just on Sunday. God says very definitely that He will deal with this because He is a jealous God who demands that His people worship Him with pure hearts. He says He will cut off those who swear by Him but also have other idols in their lives.

God says He will cut off every trace of any idol that keeps you from a life of prayer. We can go to church often, read books, listen to tapes, listen to worship music, but we don't make time to get alone with God and spend time in His presence. God is telling us that if we do not get alone with Him, He will discipline us and stir our hearts to prayer.

Unfortunately, some of us only pray when we are being disciplined by God. We are convicted and feel bad and begin to pray, and then gradually forget to pray again. The Bible says in Jeremiah 2:32, *"My people have forgotten me days without number."* It is not that you don't pray, it's that you do not have a *formal prayer time*. It is not just that you don't bow your knee to the Lord, but that you forget Him. You don't forget to pray, *you forget the Lord.* When you remember the Lord, you pray. You can't think about Him without addressing Him and adoring Him. You can't adore Him without seeking Him and you can't seek Him without praying.

Prayer comes naturally to people who remember the Lord. When we forget Him for a few days, He brings subtle, loving reminders. When we forget Him for longer periods, He begins to stir us. When we forget Him for "days without number," He brings His discipline into our personal lives and also into our nation. When a nation begins to forget about God, He stirs up that nation in a way that causes it to come back to Him and seek His face.

What God wants is very simple. He wants holy priests, devoted and single-minded worshipers, and intercessors that will seek His face day and night. He wants people who will go all-out for Him.

Calling the Intercessors

Let's consider what God does to get people in right standing with Him during times like we are living in right now. What does He do? He not only brings judgment on a nation but He raises up a small group of people called "remnant intercessors" and shines His glory on them. He reveals His heart to them and empowers them with His grace and authority. Then He causes them to model what He wants for their nation. God does not just destroy and hope something good comes of it. He always brings forth the firstfruits before He reaps the full harvest. In a time of national judgment and a need for repentance, God raises up a remnant—He raises up intercessors that have the spirit of the remnant people of God. This is the message found in chapter 2 of Zephaniah.

Some Christians want you to believe that God does not get angry and judge. They tell you that pastors who believe that God will judge our nation are un-American and unpatriotic. How could God allow an unrighteous, foreign culture to come in and do damage to a godly culture like ours? The prophet Habakkuk asked God that exact question.

"Why do You look on those who deal treacherously,
And hold Your tongue when the wicked devours one
more righteous than he?" (Habakkuk 1:13)

Here we see Habakkuk asking God how He could bring His wrath through people less holy than those being judged. How could a holy and righteous God use the actions of an unrighteous people to judge? The answer is that God loves His people and will use any tool available to remove every trace of Baal out of their lives. He will even use unrighteous people to bring forth judgment on those that appear to be more righteous. God wants to do something deeper in the heart of righteous people because He longs to raise up a holy remnant.

The first thing God says to the remnant intercessors in Zephaniah 2:1 is that they should gather themselves together. We read in Scripture that God's chosen people, the nation of Israel, had become undesirable because of their idolatry. Rather than abandoning them as a nation,

God called out a remnant that was still faithful before He unleashed the fierce anger of his righteous judgment.

Before the decree bring forth, before the day pass as the chaff, before the fierce anger of the Lord come upon you, before the day of the Lord's anger come upon you (Zephaniah 2:2 KJV).

A watchman intercessor is a person whose heart is after the Lord, seeking and worshiping Him in purity. He will understand God's heart *before* the wrath comes on the great day of the Lord. God is not talking about a *revival* here, He is talking about *judgment*. Before the judgment took place, the watchmen intercessors were already seeking and worshiping God. They were the meek of the earth who were walking in truth and righteousness.

Seek ye the Lord, all ye meek of the earth, which have wrought his judgment; seek righteousness, seek meekness: it may be ye shall be hid in the day of the Lord's anger (Zephaniah 2:3 KJV).

This verse tells us that these watchmen were the meek of the earth, a holy people in the midst of a wicked generation, who walked in truth and righteousness.

God preserves a remnant people within every generation, These people are set apart for Him and He loves them in a special way because they are seeking Him before His anger is poured out. Have you noticed what occurs in America? After something bad happens, people start seeking God and churches are filled to overflowing for a few weeks. Then when things seem to get better and people feel safer, they stop seeking Him. But remnant intercessors seek God before trouble comes. They stay on their knees before God because, like Zephaniah, they understand that the nation is no longer righteous before Him. They see that the nation is arrogant and ungodly—pastors are polluted and worship is mixed. They understand that God will judge a nation and a church in that condition, so they are on their faces praying for His mercy as He comes in wrath. They are already seeking His face as it is written three times in verse 3:

> *Seek the Lord...*
> *Seek righteousness...*
> *Seek humility...*

God is calling forth "remnant intercessors" to be true seekers of God, continually seeking Him, His righteousness, and His meekness. The prophet Isaiah says that day and night they give God no rest, continuously coming before Him in prayer interceding for mercy in the coming judgment.

We truly are living in perilous times but only the remnant intercessors understand how perilous things really are. Most people are unaware of the pending judgment we face and even believe that everything will be fine. However, remnant intercessors are on their knees before God praying that people awaken and understand their true condition.

The Bible says God does nothing without first revealing it to his prophets (see Amos 3:7). God has revealed His heart to the remnant intercessors and they are crying out to God for repentance on behalf of themselves, the nation, and the church. They are praying that God will establish a people who will seek His face, priests who are righteous, and worshipers who are pure of heart. These are people who are hungry for God, not willing that any should perish. The essence of their prayer is that God would shake this nation until people return to Him.

Zephaniah 1:12 describes those who are not fervent, watchful, remnant intercessors. They say, *"...The Lord will not do good, neither will he do evil"*

These people are spiritually complacent and unable or unwilling to see God's hand in the events taking place right before their eyes. They do not believe that these events are acts of judgment or that God would show righteous anger. "God doesn't do things like that," they say. "He won't shake anything or pour out His wrath on His people." On the other hand, they do not believe God will do anything good, either. These are people who do not believe in revival or restoration; they aren't looking for an awakening and or a mighty move of God. So they don't believe God will send revival and they don't believe He will send judgment. This means they consider God to be passive and trivial, staying in the background. When people do not believe in revival or in judgment, it's a sure sign that they are complacent at heart—not only complacent, but the Bible says they are *settled in complacency*.

The remnant intercessors are totally opposite. They are neither settled nor complacent. In fact, they are *unsettled*—and *unsettling* to those around them. The stirring in their heart prevents them from resting and losing hope. They diligently press on to know what the Lord is saying to them individually, to the church, and to the nation.

We are presented with two choices:

1. To be complacent and have a mixture in worship, allowing remnants of Baal to remain in our lives, or
2. To be watchful intercessors who are diligently seeking to know the Lord's will in the midst of trying circumstances.

When God has watchful intercessors He does something powerful! The Lord unfolds a remarkable prophecy in Zephaniah chapter 3. God does not hate you and He is not so mad that He wants to destroy you and leave you wallowing in misery. No, He wants to bring His discipline into your life so that He can raise up something mighty in your midst. He wants to do something powerful in you! However, in order to get that powerful work done, the remnant intercessors must start praying powerfully and effectively. They must know the heart of God and be a model of what God wants for the nation. Then out of the prayers and the judgment of God will come the result as stated in Zephaniah 3:8 (KJV):

Therefore wait ye upon me, saith the Lord, until the day that I rise up to the prey: for my determination is to gather the nations, that I may assemble the kingdoms, to pour upon them mine indignation, even all my fierce anger...

In this Scripture, God is admonishing watchmen

intercessors to wait on Him. He will give them an under-standing of the times even before things happen so they will know what He is up to. He will move in revival and awaken a spiritual fire in our country but He will also move in judgment and wrath. As His people wait on Him, they will get an understanding of what He is doing.

The remainder of verse 8 states, "...*for all the earth shall be devoured with the fire of my jealousy.*" Why does God bring judgment? Why would He do something that seems hurtful and destructive? Because He is a jeal-ous God! Why does He bring judgment to the church first? Because He's jealous to have a *holy people*.

Let me give you an example. I do not discipline my neighbor's children because they do not belong to me. I leave their discipline to their parents. My own children, however, are my responsibility and I discipline them. Like-wise, God says that He will bring His discipline and love to His children. He is jealous when we share our worship with idols and He is jealous that a priest would have a heart for something besides Him. He is jealous that some-body would be worshiping Him one minute and thinking of something else the next minute and worshiping it just as much. He wants single-hearted, pure devotion to Him alone. When that is not the case with His children, He allows judgment to come upon the nation with "the fire of His jealousy."

Judgment Brings Restoration

For then I will restore...(Zephaniah 3:9).

This verse brings the good news of the restoration

of His people after the fire of His jealousy. After His judgment God brings a restoration. The holy remnant intercessors are not calling for judgment but are agreeing with what God is doing in this nation. They would rather He stay His wrath and fierce anger, but they are wise enough to pray that if that is what it takes to restore His people, then that's what He must do.

Similarly, each of us needs to say, "Do what you have to do in my life to make me holy." When we say it with honesty and sincerity, we will be filled with fear and trembling. But it's a prayer we should pray because we know God is ultimately good from beginning to end and is worthy of our trust. Even what appears to us to be His anger is a fire of His jealousy to stir up our hearts so that we might be restored.

Verse 9 states, "*For then I will restore the people to a pure language…*" Language means "lips" or what they speak or specifically worship. The worship that was once mixed is now pure—to Jesus and to Jesus only. The worship that comes forth from a people who have been through the fire is pure. So God's people will have a pure language or pure worship and "*… they may all call upon the name of the Lord.*" That is pure prayer. People who have been through the refining fire of the Holy Spirit will come out as people who are washed holy and pure. They will praise God with clarity, without mixture, and they will be able to pray according to the word of the Lord.

God, who with a broken heart had to judge His people, now restores them.

The Lord thy God in the midst of thee is mighty; he

will save, he will rejoice over thee with joy; he will rest in his love, he will joy over thee with singing (Zephaniah 3:17 KJV).

God hears pure worship and sees priests who are no longer plagued with paganism. His people are no longer like the culture around them but are different and set apart. God's judgment was redemptive—the devastation worked His work! The wrath that was poured out caused a holy people to be stirred up. God says the end result is that He rejoices over us and saves us. In that day, God will sing over His people!

So we see that in these last days, God will have for Himself remnant intercessors—friends of God who are watching and seeking Him, and interceding even before the judgments come. They are examples to the world of what God desires to see in man.

Are you a remnant intercessor? Do you want God to rejoice over you? Would you like to hear God singing with joy over you? Now is the time to choose! Now is the time to act!

Blessed Are the Disruptive for They Shall Not Be Paralyzed

Now it happened on a certain day, as He was teaching, that there were Pharisees and teachers of the law sitting by, who had come out of every town of Galilee, Judea, and Jerusalem. And the power of the Lord was present to heal them. Then behold, men brought on a bed a man who was paralyzed. And they sought to bring him in and lay him before Him. And when they could not find how they might bring him in, because of the crowd, they went up on the housetop and let him down with his bed through the tiling into the midst before Jesus. So when He saw their faith, He said to him, "Man, your sins are forgiven you."

And the scribes and the Pharisees began to reason, saying, "Who is this who speaks blasphemies? Who can forgive sins but God alone?" But when Jesus perceived their thoughts, He answered and said to them, "Why are you reasoning in your hearts? Which is easier, to say, 'Your sins are forgiven you,' or to say, 'Rise up and walk'? But that you may know that the Son of Man has power on earth to forgive sins"—He said to the man who was paralyzed, "I say to you, arise, take up your bed, and go to your house." Immediately he rose up before them, took up what he had been lying on, and departed to his own house, glorifying God. And they were all amazed, and they glorified God and were filled with fear, saying, "We have seen strange things today!" (Luke 5:17-26)

In the Sermon on the Mount (Luke 6:20-22), Jesus gives a list of characteristics or activities for which one will be blessed. He speaks of blessing those who are meek, those who are poor in spirit and those who are peacemakers. This list has come to be known as "the beatitudes." However, the beatitudes did not include, "Blessed are the disruptive for they shall not be paralyzed." However, this is an attitude that Jesus not only encourages in us but one that He lived out Himself. Jesus was not only *meek and mild,* but He was *radical and wild.* On more than one occasion, Jesus was disruptive to the norms of the religious. He also was disruptive to the kingdom of darkness. His powerful life in prayer was constantly and effectively a thorn in the side of evil. When He prayed, kingdoms were moved, powers of darkness fled, and a great work of God was released on earth. He was even disruptive to those who chose to follow Him, constantly upsetting their comfort zone. When they lacked this disruptive spirit, He would come once again and awaken them to their need for vigilant, aggressive prayer, asking them, "Couldn't you fight in prayer for even an hour?" He *disruptively* turned their world upside down.

There are times in our lives when the battles we face, the tasks at hand, and the missions to which we are charged need more than casual, comfortable prayers. Comfort and ease in the sweet hour of prayer may be fine for morning devotionals, but when we are charged with a holy mission that seems totally hindered by the adversary, our true hope is found in radical, disruptive praying. Rather than a sweet hour of prayer, we often need hours of prayer, the kind that the Bible describes as "groaning."

Jesus invites us into the blessing of a disruptive life. Disruptive people challenge tradition and the status quo, often rocking the boat, asking troubling questions, praying troubling prayers, and asking God to perform things on earth that can only happen because of disruptive power from heaven. These people are often labeled radicals or troublemakers by those who do not share the same perspective or live with the same passions.

Jesus calls *all* who follow Him to be disruptive; however, many Christians are so *paralyzed* that people look at their lives and see nothing atypical or peculiar about them. We are called to be a *peculiar people* and when we are disruptive for the kingdom of God, we will appear peculiar, indeed.

Jesus said that the kingdom of God is taken by force. Those who are persistently seeking God's heart will disrupt the inertia of the kingdom of the power of darkness. The apathetic pacifist, the quiet, those low in spiritual energy, the prayerless, those who are wallowing in self-pity, or those who are paralyzed and living in fear will not be disruptive to the power of darkness, nor to the sleeping, lukewarm church. As a result, their own heart, spirit, soul, mind and body will remain paralyzed.

We live in an age in which prayerless churches need divine disruption. Sin-filled lives, unloving Christian community, and self-seeking, kingdom-building ministries are in dire need of being freed through divine disruption. Just as the paralyzed man in Luke 5 needed a miracle so, too, do the paralyzed people of God of this generation.

Jesus' Pastors' Conference

In this passage (Luke 5:17-26), Jesus was speaking in a house jam-packed with people. The house was surrounded by crowds standing around, peeking in the windows, the back door, and the front door, hoping to get a glimpse of Jesus. It was possibly the largest religious gathering that Jesus ever ministered to in a household situation. It was one of the few times where the crowd was comprised predominantly of religious leaders. The gathering was similar to a national pastors' conference today. The Bible says those in attendance came from Judea and Galilee to hear Jesus speak and teach. This was an opportunity for these men to have their lives dynamically changed forever.

These pastors had become spiritually lukewarm or even cold. To them ministry was just a job and they were like CEOs in a corporation. They had lost their prayer lives and their focus on God's heart. In their lives, the kingdom of God and the power of the Holy Spirit were secondary to church growth. This time with Jesus was an opportunity for them to get their hearts right with God. It was an opportunity for them to be stirred in their spirits, to have desperately-needed change take place in their lives. Sadly, they did not realize their need. They were leaders of churches, but they had no spiritual power and were spiritually paralyzed. Jesus longed to disrupt their wayward hearts and fruitless actions.

We see that a paralyzed man lying on a bed was brought to this meeting of religious leaders. This man is symbolic of many in the church today, not just pastors but also elders, deacons, ushers and choir members, Sunday school teachers and all Christians who serve and worship without the real power of God. They are religious but do not have the power of God living in them. They are unmoved by the Spirit of God and lie dormant on their spiritual beds. The man on the bed was physically paralyzed but the religious leaders were spiritually paralyzed. Paralyzed ministers or ministries cannot move in the Spirit of God. They can plan, purchase buildings, and grow in popularity but nothing in the realm of the Spirit is moving. It is all flesh! These so-called spiritual leaders seek ways to increase their visibility, popularity and power at the expense of love, justice and mercy. They spawn a multitude of fleshly, carnal ideas.

It is a tragedy with eternal consequences when people come to the church of God, hungry to hear His Word, and sit before a paralyzed person who is called to be their shepherd but does not teach them truth. They get cute stories, a nice, three-point sermon, or a ten-step plan on how to make life more tolerable. Recently a group of hungry believers realized they had had enough. They sat for thirty minutes while the pastor gave a sermon about how his dog was like Jesus. His dog was faithful—like Jesus; his dog was warm—like Jesus; his dog was lovable—like Jesus. And now some of his people have left his church—like Jesus!

Ezekiel 34 talks about these irresponsible shepherds.

And the word of the Lord came unto me, saying, Son of man, prophesy against the shepherds of Israel, prophesy, and say unto them, Thus saith the Lord God unto the shepherds; Woe be to the shepherds of Israel that do feed themselves! should not the shepherds feed the flocks? Ye eat the fat, and ye clothe you with the wool, ye kill them that are fed: but ye feed not the flock. The diseased have ye not strengthened, neither have ye healed that which was sick, neither have ye bound up that which was broken, neither have ye brought again that which was driven away, neither have ye sought that which was lost; but with force and with cruelty have ye ruled them.

And they were scattered, because there is no shepherd: and they became meat to all the beasts of the field, when they were scattered. My sheep wandered through all the mountains, and upon every high hill: yea, my flock was scattered upon all the face of the earth, and none did search or seek after them. Therefore, ye shepherds, hear the word of the Lord;

As I live, saith the Lord God, surely because my flock became a prey, and my flock became meat to every beast of the field, because there was no shepherd, neither did my shepherds search for my flock, but the shepherds fed themselves, and fed not my flock; Therefore, O ye shepherds, hear the word of the Lord; Thus saith the Lord God; Behold, I am against the shepherds; and I will require my flock at their hand, and cause them to cease from feeding the flock; neither shall the shepherds feed themselves any more; for I will deliver my flock from their mouth, that they may not be meat for them (Ezekiel 34:1-10 KJV).

This is a terrible accusation against men and women of God who are called to bring forth His Word. They should be teachers who are lovers of souls that rescue the lost, but instead they are concerned about themselves and how big their church is. At today's church conferences, most pastors talk about the size of their church, what their income is, and which celebrities or political leaders attend the church. God says He will take away His people from this type of shepherds because they don't have a heart for Him or for their people. God will disrupt this type of apostasy—and it is the most loving thing He could do.

I believe there is a day coming in America when God will rescue sheep out of lukewarm, half-hearted churches where the gospel is not preached and there is no prayer. He will drive His sheep out of churches that have hirelings as pastors and draw them to churches where the shepherds are after His own heart. We must not point a finger of accusation at other churches. Instead, we must examine our own hearts and carefully determine what kind of shepherds we are. Do we sometimes get this paralysis? Do we sometimes feed ourselves rather than giving to other people? God is calling us to live an "other-centered" life—giving our lives away.

These men in this account had the opportunity of a lifetime—sitting before the King of kings and the Lord of lords and hearing the word of life spoken. It could have broken their hearts and humbled them. It could have caused them to fall on their faces before Jesus and ask Him to change their lives so that He would be their all-in-all. In response to His loving disruption, they should have cried out, "Change my life, oh, God! Strip me of every-thing that does not belong in my heart. Take away all my so-called prestige, all my so-called power, and all my self-gained authority. Take it all, Jesus, because I want nothing but you and you alone." When a shepherd gets a heart like that, God moves among the sheep and some-thing powerful takes place.

These men had an opportunity to see God do some-thing miraculous in their lives and yet they were more paralyzed than the man who was let down on a bed through the roof. However, they did not recognize their paralysis. The man who could not move on the bed was constantly aware of his inability to move, but these lead-ers thought they could move—they thought they had life. They thought they could do what God was calling them to do. They thought they were obeying the commands of the Lord. They even said to Jesus, "We have followed all the commands" and Jesus told them they didn't even know they had a need.

Folks, let's put that in the context of our own lives. How many Sundays do we walk into church without receiving from Him? How many days do we miss opportunities to dig into the Word of God because we do not think we really need it? How many times do we avoid getting down on our knees or falling on our faces before the Lord? We should be saying, "God, change my life. I need you. I am hungry and thirsty for you, and I have to have you. Like Moses, I cannot go on without you. If your glory does not come, do not take me anywhere or send me anywhere. Don't do anything with me. *I want to have your glory in my life."*

They Missed Their Healing

Look at these powerful words at the end of verse 17 in Luke 5:

...and the power of the Lord was present to heal them.

Jesus was not addressing lost sheep here, or the blind and deaf, or lepers. No, He was talking to shepherds, the spiritual leaders, who needed healing. Shepherds of the church need to look at their own hearts. As we sit before Jesus, His power is present to heal but do we recognize our need? Do we humbly and hungrily cry out to God and acknowledge our need? Can we pray the words of one of the old hymns?

Pass me not, O gentle Savior, Hear my humble cry;

While on others Thou art calling, Do not pass me by.

Fanny J. Crosby, 1820-1915

Unfortunately, many of us today do not think like that. We are more like the proud man Jesus observed praying in the temple, "Lord, I thank you that I am not like these poor sinners who have so many needs." Those of us who call ourselves Christians sometimes come to believe we are able to stand before God simply because we are religious (i.e., we open a Bible or go to a worship service). We raise our hands, lift our heads, and say, "Thank you, God, that I am not like the sinners." If we do this, we will miss the powerful opportunity when the power of the Lord is present to heal us.

Let me ask you some very important questions:

- Are there areas of your heart, soul, mind, or body that need to be healed?
- Do you have an emotional struggle?
- Do you have a relational struggle?
- Is there a burden in your life that has caused you to be weighed down by a particular habit of sin?
- Have you lost your passion for Jesus or forgotten God for days?

If you can answer "yes" to any of these, the Lord says you have a need and until you are aware of your need, healing will not take place.

Sadly, the men who witnessed the healing of the paralyzed man missed it. The word "paralyzed" in Webster's Dictionary is defined as: *to make powerless or ineffective, to live in a state of powerlessness.* These men were spiritually paralyzed.

Have you ever walked in spiritual paralysis—what could be termed a "spiritual haze"—of your soul? You may recognize the symptoms:

- dullness of your mind
- a fog over your eyes
- a lack of passion in your life
- a prayerless existence

You sense a spiritual hunger. You want the Holy Spirit to fill your life so that you live and move in Christ, but instead you yawn and settle for mere existence. This is spiritual paralysis.

Do you open up the Word of God to a particular book and think you've already read that portion a dozen times, so you turn on over to John, then Acts and so on? Do you keep doing this until you eventually conclude that there's nothing new in the Scriptures for you? When we are in a spiritual haze, we can read the Word for 15 or 20 minutes and then not remember a thing we just read.

When our "spiritual paralysis" is healed through repentance and the power is restored, any page in the Bible can speak ten sermons to us. The entire Word of God comes alive and amazing revelations come to those who have been disrupted from their slumber. The problem is that many of us are like these Pharisees. We are spiritually paralyzed, numb, dull and lifeless and there is no fruit in our lives. We go on like this day after day, month after month, without recognizing or admitting our paralysis and our need for help. The sad thing is that the power of the Lord was available to the Pharisees—and it is available to us! Jesus is right here now to disrupt our lives—but we cannot be healed if we sit passively and refuse to ask for help.

Spiritual *paralysis* can cause chronic spiritual *laziness* but that does not necessarily mean that you are not *religious*. The leaders in Luke 5 were doing all the right "religious stuff" and adhering to all the rules and regulations. Still their priorities were wrong and they were apathetic regarding spiritual matters, pursuing outward things while remaining unclean. Jesus told them that they were missing the core of the gospel—love and mercy. He went on to tell them that they were just bones, with no life in them. Those Pharisees left Jesus' presence without having their paralysis healed. The sad part of the story is that the power of the Lord was there.

If Jesus said to you, "I am here to heal. I am here to wake you up and disrupt your life. I want to turn you upside down and shake you from your toes to your head," how do you think you would respond? How unspeakably sad to be in His presence and hear Him speak, then just sit passively and answer, "Oh, I don't know. I'm not sure I need that right now." This form of spiritual paralysis isn't produced by a fall or a jolt to the system but through endless lack of movement where atrophy of the spirit sets in and takes hold.

Slothfulness casteth into a deep sleep; and an idle soul shall suffer hunger (Proverbs 19:15 KJV).

The hunger referred to in verse 15 is what we experience when we are too lazy or too "paralyzed" to wake up to get food. Jesus wants us to awaken from our sleep and stop being lazy, as we see expressed even stronger in verse 24.

A slothful man hideth his hand in his bosom, and will not so much as bring it to his mouth again (Proverbs 19:24 KJV).

If a man has a bowl of food before him and won't even feed himself, *that's lazy!* The same applies in the spiritual sense. You're hungry and a "bowl of food" is put in front of you, but you're too lazy to dig in. You don't even put the food into your mouth. You go to church and the Word is there but you don't partake. The Word could nourish, fill and change you, but you won't take it into your heart.

It has been said that *you are what you eat* but more accurately, you are what you absorb and assimilate. Are you changed when you take in God's Word? The Scriptures must be spiritually comprehended before they can convey God's life-giving power to you. What about when you pray? When the Holy Spirit breaks our spiritual paralysis, suddenly prayer will seem like the choicest of foods and every page of God's Word will come alive. New revelation will be poured out to you and you will be able to partake of the life that God is offering to you.

They Sought

What should you do with your spiritual paralysis—those times when you can't seem to move spiritually and the life of God is not moving you? What did the men in Luke 5 do? The Bible says the friends of the paralyzed man "… *sought*…" which means "to bring him in." This is a persistent seeking that would not be stopped and these men were not deterred by obstructions and difficulties. Just as they sought Jesus to cure their paralyzed friend, so must we seek the Lord for the cure for our spiritual paralysis. Seek the Lord to supply your lack, even during times when you don't know what you need. God stirs up our hearts when we seek Him.

Some believers seem to think that God has preordained how much of His presence each of us will receive regardless of what we do. They think we won't receive more by seeking or less by being apathetic. I don't believe that at all. I believe you can get as much of Jesus as you want. I believe hungry hearts get more of Jesus than those who are slothful. I believe people who are desperate for God get fed more from Him than those who are half-hearted. And I believe you find Him based on the degree that you seek after Him.

Jesus says:

> Seek me and you will find;
> Knock and it will be opened;
> Ask and you shall receive.

If people do not seek, knock and ask, they will not be healed of their spiritual paralysis.

The paralytic's friends were Kingdom-Seekers who would not be denied when the door would not open up to them because of the crowd. They were seeking a miracle. They knew the power and life of Jesus was in the house and they were determined to enter into His presence. They didn't give up and rationalize by saying, "God must not have wanted our friend to get his miracle."

No! These men refused to be minimized by obstacles and difficulties. They cried out for the awakening of their friend just as we need to cry out for a spiritual awakening in the church. We must pray every day that Christians will get into the presence of Jesus. Make this your prayer: *"Burn the passion of Jesus in our souls, oh, God. Help us not to be satisfied unless we have all of you. God, stir our hearts to be seekers of your face and your hand and your kingdom. Let us be disruptive people to the world around us. Let us shake kingdoms through your power and your glory—and let me be part of it."*

How many of us pray like that? We may hear God telling us to do something but when it doesn't work the first time we try it, we doubt whether God was really in it. We figure we must have tried to act in our flesh. We interpret obstacles as God's way of closing the door. *"God seems to have closed the door on that one."* How many times have you heard Christians say that? It's true that God sometimes closes the door (and this calls for spiritual discernment), but you can only have discernment if you are alive and not suffering from paralysis. If you're alive in Christ, you can distinguish between the voice of God and the acts of the enemy.

Satan is the "Master of Paralysis." As soon as an opportunity knocks on your door, he suggests that you are not supposed to do this or that. He may drop doubt that God would never have called you to do a certain thing because you're not submissive or powerful enough. Just as quickly as you have that thought, The Master of Paralysis will begin to try to convince you that you can't do it. "You tried to be an overcomer, but you failed. You tried to get in the front door to minister but you couldn't."

You need to be like the men in Luke 5. If the front door is blocked, then go to the back door. I can almost see these men grab that pallet with the paralyzed man and go around back. But what if the back door is just as jam-packed as the front door? Well, Satan always has an answer. He may suggest that you tried two times without success, so it's pretty obvious that God wasn't in it.

If we believe Satan's lies, we may begin to compromise on God's call and fail to move powerfully ahead with His purpose for us. We might even be tempted to settle for second-best by saying, "We tried the front and we tried the back, and obviously this is not working." Then we begin to rationalize and moderate our goals. The friends of the paralyzed man could have done this. "Did you see the schedule? I think Jesus is going to be back next week, isn't He? We can just come back next week. After all, this man has been paralyzed for thirty years—he can wait one more week." If we are not willing to be disruptive and are instead easily discouraged and hindered, we will be disappointed when we seek something. Then eventually we just stop seeking things from God and become spiritually paralyzed.

When You Can't Find a Way

And when they could not find by what way they might bring him in because of the multitude, they went upon the housetop, and let him down through the tiling with his couch into the midst before Jesus (Luke 5:19 KJV).

The friends of the paralytic left us a powerful example of not becoming paralyzed in spite of multiple obstacles. Many of us get to the point this man's friends reached. Perhaps our obstacle is an emotional heartache so extreme that we stop reading the Bible and praying or, in extreme cases, even leave the church. We try everything we can think of but when nothing seems to work we just give up.

In the midst of difficulties, hardships, and obstacles, we must remember that the strongest attacks of Satan are directed at those who diligently and persistently seek God. If our relationship with Him is distant because we are not seeking Him, or if we are spiritually paralyzed, Satan will probably not bother us much. However, the moment we start to seek Him wholeheartedly, Satan puts up barriers. We must not give up or we will miss the powerful release that the Holy Spirit has for us—and that's what Satan wants!

In the face of obstacles, the paralytic's friends did not give up; instead, they became *disruptive* and knocked a hole through the roof. I don't know how they did it but I'm sure it wasn't done quietly and orderly. I'm certain the noise, the falling dust, and the debris thoroughly disrupted the gathering in the house. They didn't say, "Oh, let's quietly remove this tile so we won't disturb anyone." No, I think they stomped around and removed whatever they needed to without regard to the commotion they caused. Jesus taught, "Blessed are the meek," while the boom-boom of a sledgehammer is heard. Pieces of the roof start to fall and dust fills the room as "Blessed are the poor in spirit" is heard. Then suddenly a hole appears in the roof and the crowd backs away, surprised to see a man on a bed being lowered into their midst.

The Pharisees were startled but Jesus knew what was happening and probably just smiled. I can imagine that He was thinking, "This is great! These Pharisees have been sitting here listening to all I've said, turning a deaf ear. They are as paralyzed as when they came in—and they'll still be paralyzed when they leave unless they change. I think they may be ready for something new to take place. I can hardly wait to see this person come down."

The men on the roof were saying by their actions, "Here we come, Jesus! We're coming! We couldn't get through the front door or the back door or the window, but we're not stopping. We are *determined* to get to you."

Most of us have been taught to pray for Jesus to *come to us* when we have a need, but is God calling us instead to *come to Him*, to seek Him with a whole heart? It requires a shift in thinking to move from asking the Lord to rend the heavens and come down to realizing that the Lord is telling us to "rend the roof" and diligently *seek Him*. The power of the Lord is available to heal, so why don't we come to Him? *Why don't we run to Him?* Why don't we knock down doors, kick in windows, and break through roofs to get to Him? What keeps us from being as bold and disruptive as the paralytic's friends?

My message to you is, "Blessed are the disruptive." Too many pastors spend their time encouraging people not to be disruptive. "Stay calm, don't go to extremes, be sensible," they say. A majority of pastors in America today want things done "with decency and order." Solomon wrote, *"You can have a clean barn but there won't be any oxen in it" (Proverbs 14:4).* What he means is that things can be clean and tidy but the purpose of the barn, the reason the barn exists, is to house oxen. Some people keep the oxen away so that the barn stays clean—but empty!

I want to invite you to be disruptive. Get a little rowdy! Ask great things from Jesus and seek Him with abandoned passion. The Bible invites you to press on, dig in, get disruptive, and refuse to settle for the status quo. Refuse to be robbed by Satan, the liar who tells you that you cannot be saved or have freedom. Squelch his voice with persistence and single-mindedness because you *can* get more from God and be an overcomer.

My prayer is that God will awaken you to paralysis and stir your heart to be alive in Him. This spiritual apathy must be disrupted. You may have been religious all your life, just playing spiritual games. If this is true, it is time to do something new. If you keep repeating the same thing over and over and it's not working, do something new! Throw yourself at the feet of Jesus and say, "Jesus, the power to heal is with you and if I have to break through the roof to get to you, that's what I'll do because I need your life."

I say unto thee, Arise, and take up thy couch, and go into thine house. And immediately he rose up...(Luke 5:24-25).

The paralytic's spiritual paralysis was cured by Jesus' words, "Man, thy sins are forgiven thee." His physical paralysis was cured when Jesus said just one word, "*Arise!*" What do you need to free you from your paralysis? All you have to do is draw near to Him and listen to Him, and then His Word will come to you!

After the paralytic was with Jesus, his neighbors saw a radically changed man. They saw the glory of God in his life. When Jesus sets a person free from spiritual paralysis, watch out! Those people are going to make an impact on the kingdom of God. They will appear a little different by the world's standards, even appearing irrational, unpredictable, and strange. People who are filled with the Holy Spirit are strange *in a good way*.

You have a choice. Do you want to be disruptive? Perhaps you prefer to conform and fit in with the crowd. You'd rather follow religious tradition by coming to church once a week and fulfilling your religious duty. If that is all you want then you will be like the Pharisees and stay in your paralysis. If you want more of Him, if you want to come alive, if you want to take up your bed of paralysis and walk, run, and dance, Jesus will meet you and heal your paralysis.

Into the Secret Place

And when you pray, you shall not be like the
hypocrites. For they love to pray standing in the
synagogues and on the corners of the streets, that
they may be seen by men. Assuredly, I say to you,
they have their reward. But you, when you pray, go
into your room, and when you have shut your door,
pray to your Father who is in the secret place; and
your Father who sees in secret will reward you openly.

But when you pray, do not use vain repetitions as
the heathen do. For they think that they will be heard
for their many words. Therefore do not be like them.
For your Father knows the things you have need of
before you ask Him (Matthew 6:5-8).

Many churchgoers see prayer as a positive activity.
They like the idea of prayer and want to become prayers. But just loving prayer is not what Jesus wants. At-
tending prayer seminars and conferences, reading books
on prayer, and even praying every once in awhile is not
what God calls us to. In the above passage about prayer,

Jesus talks to the religious leaders, the Pharisees, and calls them hypocrites. The Pharisees outwardly followed a religious system but did not have a heart after God. They loved to pray, but only because they wanted to be seen by others.

Jesus is very clear about the various motivations for prayer. He pointed out that although the Pharisees loved to pray, there was something missing. They didn't pray in the secret place and fervently seek God's heart. Their prayers were not separated from the world. There was no communion with the Father, no fellowship. Theirs were simply words. I could shout "hallelujah" a thousand times and if my heart was in it, God would appreciate every one. If I didn't mean the praise, it would merely be vain repetition, as we saw in Chapter One.

What makes a prayer vain in God's eyes? In this passage, Jesus says, "It's in vain because you are not in the secret place and your repetition has no connection to Me. You are still counting on your own understanding, living in your own world, depending on your own power, trusting your own ingenuity, and seeking after fame and fortune. All you are doing is *reciting* prayers. You have to leave that world and get into *My* world. Come into My secret place. You must exit *that* place and enter My secret place. Shut the door behind you, lock it, get on your knees and begin to seek My face."

Of course, this doesn't mean that you can only pray by yourself behind closed doors. Actually, you can pray in your car, or on the street or in church, because Jesus is not concerned about our *physical location* when we pray—He's referring to a heart attitude. Jesus prayed in synagogues, in gardens, out in the desert and on streets. When sick and desperately needy people ran to Him crying for help, He didn't ask them to come indoors and get into a closet. He doesn't care where we pray but He clearly doesn't want our motivation to be self-centered. We're not to pray merely to be seen by men. Praying in public should not be done to receive credit or reward from men. Our heart must be in communion with God "in the secret place" even though physically we may be in a public place.

He Sees in Secret

We need to understand the depth and power of what Jesus is saying in Matthew 6:6 when He talks about the Father seeing in secret. We may pray religious prayers hoping to be seen as a wonderful saint, but God not only doesn't hear those prayers, He doesn't even notice we're praying. Since He sees "in secret," He only sees us or hears us when our hearts are in communion with Him in the secret place of His heart. He will only glance upon, look toward, and give favor to that which transpires in the heart of the secret place. Yes, that can be on the streets but the prayer must come from communion with Him, not from a desire to demonstrate our eloquence and passion or to make a show of our faith. It is entrance into the realm of the Spirit and not just a physical room that Jesus is talking about here. It's His place, and when you get there He sees you. He doesn't see your fleshly efforts— in fact, He ignores them.

When Jesus sees you seeking Him, you win His heart. Song of Solomon 4:9 (Amp.) says that with just one glance we have won His heart. Some people have worked hard in the flesh and have yet to sense God's favor, but those who meet Him in His secret place and move out into works of love are constantly under His eyes and care.

Where do you find this kind of love from Jesus? Where do you get His glance and His favor? Only in the secret place! Are you running around striving to be seen by men, trying to be recognized and honored? Are you seeking prestige and power, hoping that people will pat you on the back for doing such a "wonderful job"? One day you will stand before the Father and say, "Didn't we do all these wonderful things in your name?" Sadly, He will say, "No, I didn't see that; I didn't know you were dong that. I saw people who were seeking My face. They were healing, preaching, and loving the lost but I didn't see you do that." Why not? Because you weren't in His presence! You were doing everything in your own power and energy, trying to manipulate something or gain favor or earn something from God and man.

The Father's eyes of favor are not on the worldly-wise men of power and eloquence. The Father sees those who are humble in Spirit and doing the works of Jesus out of a simple love for Him. They have been transformed *in His presence* and now they are so much like Jesus that they are doing amazing deeds.

When you get into that secret place, you begin to see things from God's perspective. You see the hurts of the world—people who are brokenhearted, whose marriages are failing, and who are lonely, depressed, suicidal, and on drugs. If you were to pass them on the street or casually speak to them at church on Sunday morning without having been with God, you might think that they were the happiest people in the world. But when you have been in God's presence, you see through His eyes. As you walk down that same street and see the same people, you see them with new eyes. Tears of compassion will even sting your eyes as you view the world around you through the Father's eyes.

Secretly Together

We can pray alone in many places: at home, in our cars, walking down streets or through malls and airports. The 120 gathered in The Upper Room were together but they were also in the secret place with Him. Why? Because they were in the place where God wanted them and He "saw" them there and met with them. God also calls the church to join our hearts together in corporate prayer. He challenges us as a church to enter into that secret room as a body, rather than stay isolated in a room by ourselves.

If we don't get on fire for God alone, we may need to get in a place where someone else is on fire and catch a little bit of what they have. You can get into the secret place with God when others are in the room even though it may be more difficult because of distractions.

Community prayer meetings can encourage us. You may get tired of praying but when you are with others who are praying with passion, fire, and zeal, your desire for prayer revives and you want what they have. Be sure you don't join in with a carnal attitude, because that will diminish the power of the Spirit in the meeting.

Some people get off track when it comes to prayer because they haven't been in the secret place. Instead of being intimate with God they build fanciful and ridiculous man-made structures and develop systems of prayer. It would be much better if we did as the disciples did and ask Jesus to teach us how to pray. Too much attention to instruction and administration can complicate our prayer life. There are too many carnal ideas that can get our attention and divert us from His heart. That is exactly why Jesus condemned the Pharisees and called them hypocrites.

Standing in the Gap

God says He is looking for someone who is willing to "stand in the gap," that wide, empty place where something is missing. What is the gap in many churches today? Evangelism, worship, teaching, preaching, good works, Sunday school, and youth ministry are well covered, but your church's "gap" may be prayer. The Lord calls His church to stand in the gap—not jump over the gap, or pass by the gap, or go to a seminar on the gap, or read a book about the gap—but to *stand in the gap*, no matter what the outcome might be.

If you pray only to get success in your own life, you are just like the Pharisees—and Jesus called them hypocrites or pretenders. You pretend to stand in the gap for somebody else but really you want something for yourself. If you don't get what you want from God after fifteen minutes, you quit praying. The prayer meeting and seeking His face are no longer a part of your life—and you now doubt that God will answer prayer.

God seeks persistent, faithful, heart-felt prayer. Standing in the gap in the secret place with God for fifteen minutes each day is a good start. You will find those fifteen minutes turn to twenty and then thirty. Don't worry about how long you pray, just be consistent. Your joy of prayer will become so overwhelming that the time will increase naturally.

God is looking for even one pray-er with the correct motive. When you get in that secret place, what do you want the Father to see? Do you want him to see somebody who is cantankerous and cranky? I'm sure you would much rather have Him see someone patient who says, "Father, I set my face toward you. I want to know you and love you and love others as you love them."

The Bible clearly tells us He wants us to be filled with His love and power—and this only happens when we go into the secret place with Him. If you are doing good works just to be seen by men, that's all you will see—and your life will become consumed with questions. "Did they see me? Do they appreciate what I've done? Am I accepted? Am I loved?" When you are standing in the gap and serving Him, it won't matter what others say and you won't be looking for that pat on the back, because the Father's eyes are on you and He is saying, "Well done, good and faithful servant."

The Secret Place Reveals *Your Secret Heart*

God reveals your secret heart *to you* when you spend time with Him in the secret place. At other times you are too busy *doing* to hear Him. You may be surprised at what He reveals to you; recognizing pettiness, selfishness, deceitfulness, and carnality in your heart can be very painful and unpleasant. Even though God may convict and rebuke you in secret, that's better than being exposed in public. God is merciful and when He confronts, He also redeems and restores if you're repentant.

Let's go one step further. It is better to have God reveal the secrets of your heart here than to stand before Him at the believers' judgment. This is where good works done by fleshly power will be burned up like wood, hay and straw. The disillusionment now will be more tolerable than the surprise and disappointment then.

Unless you go into the secret place with the Lord now, you may have many tears for Him to wipe away when you stand before Him in judgment. Get into the secret place and ask the Father to show you your heart. Cry out to Him, "Reveal my heart to me. Show me my wicked ways. Tell me now so that I may change."

The heart is deceitful above all things, And desperately wicked... I, the LORD, search the heart, I test the mind... (Jeremiah 17:9-10).

God searches all things—including our hearts. He says He loves to reveal His secrets to those who seek His face, so get into that secret place with Him.

The Secret Place Reveals *His* Secret Heart

God will reveal your own heart to you. As you repent, your heart is cleansed and you become His whole, pure, and spotless Bride. But there's another side to this.

Not only does He reveal the secrets of your heart, but He loves to reveal the secrets of His heart to you when you meet Him in the secret place. He will tell you about Himself and reveal to you His love, power, goodness, and grace. The more time you spend in His presence the more revelation of Him you will receive.

The church culture in America today knows a lot about keeping rules and doing "ten steps…" to one thing or another. We are taught how to work, how to get our marriages straight, how to raise our kids and how to tithe. We know *"how to"* but too many of us don't know the secrets of the Father's heart.

You may be able to echo famous Christian leaders and best-selling authors. However, when you receive truth from God's heart and share it, people will be touched because it will be fresh and new. You are given these secrets for yourself but what you learn is so rich that you want to share with others. These revelations from God's heart are hard to keep secret.

For your Father knows the things you have need of before you ask Him (Matthew 6:8).

If God already knows what we are going to ask Him before we even get to the secret place, why go there? Because, even though you know your need, you don't know what He is going to say to you—you don't know His heart until He reveals it to you. God wants to share His heart; in fact, He tells us, "I've been looking for a man—I've been looking for a woman. With whom can I share my heart? Who will wait on me, listen to me?" A.W. Tozer wrote that God speaks to the man who listens—and

He's looking for those who are willing to spend time with Him and hear His voice.

This presents another challenge. Do you listen for God's voice when you're in His presence? Sadly, when we get into the secret place with Him, we usually *don't* listen. Instead, we engage in one-sided conversations. We pray about our finances, our family, our marriage, and our jobs until our prayers become little more than a list of worries. When this happens, we aren't really praying at all. God counsels us to spend less time asking for things and more time listening to Him. When we're in God's presence, two things happen:

- He reveals your heart to you so that you can know yourself better
- He reveals His heart to you so that you can know who He is

A person who doesn't enter that secret place might pray for long periods of time and even do many charitable deeds, but he already has his reward here on earth…just like the Pharisees did. Sometimes it might be difficult to do your charitable deeds in secret and this seems to contradict the teaching of Matthew 5:16, *"Let your light so shine before men, that they may see your good works and glorify your Father in heaven."*

While this may seem confusing, I believe Jesus is referring to our *motive* for doing good works, not necessarily how we physically do them. God looks at the heart and if our motives are right, then we are working in the Spirit, not in the flesh to be seen and rewarded by men. The Spirit of Jesus compels us to do His works and our motives will be pure when we have been with Him. This same principle is true when it pertains to fasting; we must not fast to impress men but to obey and please God.

Several years ago when I was living in New York City, a young homeless man came into my office. He was worn out and beaten down, and his shoes were ripped to shreds. I had on a wonderful pair of cowboy boots my wife had bought for me in Texas. I had worn them just long enough to make them fit perfectly and comfortably. When I noticed this young man's feet, I felt the Holy Spirit lead me to give him my boots. I obeyed the voice of the Spirit—then he walked out wearing my boots—and I walked out in socks!

About six months later I received a phone call from a friend in North Carolina. "Hey, Gary, you're not going to believe this. I have a guy here in my office who is entering our drug rehab program. Do you know the reason he gave for coming to us? He said, 'Six months ago in New York City I sat in the office of a pastor named Gary Wilkerson. He gave me his cowboy boots and I've been walking around in them ever since. I've gone from city to city doing drugs and drinking as much as possible, but I couldn't get over the fact that somebody loved me enough to take off his own boots and give them to me.'" That day that young man entered a wonderful Christian rehab program.

Now my friend knew I had done a charitable deed. Did I end that conversation thinking that I had lost my reward because someone knew what I had done? If that's the case, then I've *really* lost my reward now, because I've just told everyone who reads this.

But no! That's not what Jesus is talking about here in Matthew 5. He's not saying that every gift, every act of kindness and deed of love must be done in hidden places where absolutely no one can know. The powerful truth Jesus is showing us here is that our works of love are established in the secret place—not when you actually *do* a certain thing. You found the Father's heart and His love when you knelt and said, "God, I *must* know your heart. I must know your compassion and your love." And in that place He fills your heart with His love and His direction. With His eyes you see what needs to be done. This is why Jesus could say, "I only do what I see the Father doing."

"...They have their reward..." (Matthew 6:2). Jesus said that those who do charitable deeds or fast to be seen of men already have the reward of appearing righteous before men, but *they don't have His reward.* I don't want congratulations and pats on the back—I want His reward, His presence and blessing on my life. No person on earth can truly reward me. You might be nice, loving, powerful or popular and I might admire and respect you, but you can't deeply satisfy my soul. Human rewards are temporal, fleshly, and earthly, but Jesus' rewards are spiritual and eternal. He alone can bring life, mercy, wisdom and true riches. Which do you choose?

> *When Elisha came into the house, there was the child, lying dead on his bed. He went in therefore, shut the door behind the two of them, and prayed to the Lord. And he went up and lay on the child, and put his mouth on his mouth, his eyes on his eyes, and his*

hands on his hands; and he stretched himself out on the child, and the flesh of the child became warm. He returned and walked back and forth in the house, and again went up and stretched himself out on him; then the child sneezed seven times, and the child opened his eyes (2 Kings 4:32-35).

This account of the prophet Elisha reviving a dead child could be viewed as a parable. Elisha represents Jesus and the dead child represents us, although we are spiritually dead rather than physically dead. Jesus sees our spiritual condition like Elisha saw the physical condition of the boy. We are spiritually dead to the passion, joy, zeal and life of prayer and intimacy that He calls us to. "He [Elisha] went in therefore, shut the door behind the two of them...." Elisha and this young man were in the secret place, the same place Jesus wants to take us in our need. Life springs forth in that secret place! We may try harder and redouble our efforts, but it will never work. You can't redouble the efforts of a dead man! You must have life.

Jesus calls us into this place of life in Revelation 3:20.

Behold, I stand at the door, and knock: if any man hear my voice, and open the door, I will come in to him, and will sup with him, and he with me (KJV).

When Jesus "knocks," He is asking His church to come into the secret place with Him in order to receive His life. He will revive us, just as Elisha revived the boy. The boy was already in the room and he needed the one with the power to enter the room and bring life. When Jesus asks us "to open that He might come in," He is saying He wants to awaken our deadened hearts. It is in this inner chamber with Him that we come to life.

Draw near to God, and he will draw near to you…
(James 4:8).

We like to feel the Lord drawing near before we enter into the secret place, but the Word tells us here that we are to draw near to Him. In other words, sometimes we have to make the first move and get in a place of receptivity. We sometimes say to God, "You draw me and I'll respond to you." James is telling us that we need to do just the opposite: "You go to Him and wait for Him until He reveals Himself to you." We can say to Jesus, "Here I am, standing in need of you. I know you're always with me but I'm asking for a deeper revelation of your presence in order that I might have abundant life. I'm here in this room and I've shut the door as a sign that I'm not going anywhere. I won't leave until I hear that knock."

Elisha knocked on the door where the young boy was and stretched himself over him. Warmth came to the boy, and then eventually life returned! Jesus works with us in the same manner. He puts His eyes on our eyes because He wants us to see what He sees—His mouth on ours that we may learn to speak what He speaks—His heart on ours so we will feel what He feels. He touches our hands and feet because He wants us to work the works that He does and walk where He walks. Like that child, something stirs in our hearts, we get spiritually warmer, and life comes into us!

It may seem that God walks away for a while. In

verse 35 we read: *"He [Elisha] returned and walked back and forth in the house, and again went up and stretched himself out on him; then the child sneezed seven times and the child opened his eyes."* Perhaps interruptions come to test our faith, but will we wait upon the Lord to renew our strength? Like Elisha returned to the boy, God will return to us.

You may feel spiritually dead, but are you patiently and fervently awaiting the life-giving touch of the Lord? Do you go into the secret place where Jesus can put His life in you and warm your heart and soul? Without His life in you, you grow cold so quickly. One day goes by and you begin to get cool; two days pass and religious rigor mortis starts to set in—you get spiritually stiff and cold. That's why Jesus says, "Come into My presence every day. Seek My face daily—not weekly, not occasionally, but *every day*." Stand in that gap!

Run for More of Jesus

But the angel answered and said to the women, "Do not be afraid, for I know that you seek Jesus who was crucified. He is not here; for He is risen, as He said. Come, see the place where the Lord lay. And go quickly and tell His disciples that He is risen from the dead, and indeed He is going before you into Galilee; there you will see Him. Behold, I have told you." So they went out quickly from the tomb with fear and great joy, and ran to bring His disciples word. And as they went to tell His disciples, behold, Jesus met them, saying, "Rejoice!" So they came and held Him by the feet and worshiped Him (Matthew 28:5-9).

Now Thomas, called the Twin, one of the twelve, was not with them when Jesus came. The other disciples therefore said to him, "We have seen the Lord." So he said to them, "Unless I see in His hands the print of the nails, and put my finger into the print of the nails, and put my hand into His side, I will not believe" (John 20:24-25).

These two passages of Scripture present a study in sharp contrast between the heart attitude of Mary and the apostle Thomas. This contrast is similar to the dual nature in each of us. Sometimes we seek Jesus with a whole heart and long to be in His presence. We run to Him in prayer and seek intimacy with Him. At other times we drift away because we lack a passion for Him. Our hearts grow cold, our faith becomes stale, and our prayers dry up. At such times we may drift into a carelessness that causes us to stop showing up altogether. We might even forget Him for long periods of time.

Let's look at these two characters:

1. Mary—she was passionate for Jesus, running to the tomb early in the morning
2. The apostle Thomas—he chose not to be present at the time of Jesus' revelation of Himself

In these two followers of Christ, we have a perfect example of people who have differing hearts. One is on fire and longs to know more of God. The other no longer has a fervency for God and has lost touch with Him. In each of these characters we can find a little of ourselves. The Bible says these things were written for our example, so let's examine Mary and Thomas and study the contrast between their heart attitudes toward Jesus.

Complacent Believer

First, let's look again at John 20:24:

Now Thomas, called the Twin, one of the twelve, was not with them when Jesus came.

Thomas is commonly known as Doubting Thomas because he had trouble believing that Jesus truly had risen from the dead. Today almost every time his name is mentioned, the word "doubt" is attached to it. He would not believe unless he could physically touch the scars on Jesus' body.

The fact that Thomas doubted is troubling, but more troubling is the fact that he chose to be absent from the other apostles. Perhaps a better name for him would be "Thomas the Absent" or "Thomas—the one who is missing out." He missed great blessings because he didn't give himself the opportunity to be in the presence of Jesus. His doubt would have diminished if he had been there when Jesus walked through the closed door. That miracle was enough to make even a skeptic believe. Thomas missed out because he didn't show up!

We say we want to learn to pray but we don't go to prayer meetings. We say we love His presence but then ignore Him for days. We say we are hungry for a word from God but hardly ever open His Word. We say we want to intercede for others but we allow ourselves to become distracted by the busy-ness of our lives. We run here and there, charging ahead, crossing off items from our to-do list, all the while missing out on Jesus.

Thomas apparently had only a casual commitment to Jesus and didn't pursue Him with a whole heart. Seeking Jesus was not his highest priority or, as we might say today, it was not "job one." Thomas' casual commitment caused him to become lukewarm and he began to drift.

Like Thomas, we will begin to drift if we seek Jesus

by sight rather than by faith. At times we will feel His touch but we can't wait for that to happen before we connect with Him. We can't wait for the emotional experience of a divine encounter—we must come to Him every day.

Jesus wants to meet with each of you daily, not just on Sunday or in other church services. He longs to be with you all day long—when you awaken in the morning until you go to sleep at night. He wants you to breathe Him in, walk alongside Him and talk with Him. That's how you will get to know Him well—and when you think you know Him as well as you possibly could, He invites you to know Him even better.

Thomas wasn't just "Doubting Thomas," he was "Absent Thomas" and because of this, his unbelief overshadowed his faith. He was like the Israelites in the Old Testament, who broke God's heart because they forgot Him for days and weeks. He lost his hunger for intimacy with Jesus, so he couldn't feel His touch, hear His voice or feel His presence. He may have been waiting for Jesus to do something miraculous, like appearing in the clouds, to let everyone know He was alive. Sadly, Thomas was waiting for *Jesus* to move while *he* stood completely still.

Some people aren't faithful when God seems distant or absent. Their attitude is, "If God isn't coming through for me, I'll just go my own way until He begins to move again." We can't force God to keep us on an emotional high. If we only seek Him when we *feel* Him, we're going to miss a lot of Him!

Even though I was brought up in a Christian home, I

went through a period of doubt. My father is a pastor and evangelist—my grandfather was a pastor—my great-grandfather was an evangelist—and my great-great-grandfather was a chaplain in the Civil War. I certainly should have had a sure foundation in faith, but when I was seventeen years old I became an agnostic. I studied the Baha'i faith and it sounded good to me because it taught that all roads lead to God. God is on top of the mountain and Christians come up one way, Buddhists come up another way, and Muslims come up yet another way—any way is fine as long as God is on the top.

...I am the way, the truth and the life. No one comes to the Father except through Me (John 14:6).

I started examining the faith of my childhood and Jesus became a stumbling block. He was either a liar or a lunatic. He either didn't deserve to be believed or He was telling the truth—I had a choice to make. At seventeen years of age I went through this crisis of doubt and faith. How could I know for sure? I was a confused young man.

One day as I was praying, Jesus made His presence known to me. I fell to my knees and the glory of the Lord filled the room. It was not physically illuminating but there was a light in my soul. It was made clear to me that Jesus Christ was my savior and friend. I knew He was alive! I knew He lived in my heart—He ruled and reigned and loved me and poured out His Spirit on me. From that moment on I had no more doubt. I knew that I didn't have to search world religions or study history anymore. My search was over *because I knew Him.*

If you are like Thomas and don't pursue Jesus, you're going to miss the experience of being in His presence. This will lead to doubt and no matter how many counselors you consult or self-help books you read, you won't find the answer you're looking for. Every supposed answer you receive will only cause more questions. However, once you are in the presence of Jesus, grace, life, and power will enter your soul and your basic questions about life will be answered!

Missing the opportunity to strengthen his faith in Jesus' presence caused Thomas to grow lukewarm. As he lost his zeal, he became more complacent and was willing to settle for less of Jesus. Similarly, you also have a choice! Will you settle for less of the glory of God or will you covet more of Him and strive to appropriate all that He offers you?

You must be greedy for Jesus. If you can't find what you want in a church service, then seek for it by yourself—one-on-one with Him. You *must* have His presence. Don't think you can wait until you hear just the right sermon or the right song in the right environment. Believe me, such a place does not exist—because nothing is right unless He is present.

Missing His Presence, Missing His Peace

What do you miss when Jesus is not present? *Peace!* Jesus loves and accepts you and this brings peace. Thomas didn't have peace, because he was spiritually indifferent. Jesus will listen to you, accept you and love you— and this produces peace. Thomas did not have that. He missed the security, hope, and power of God when his life could have been filled with joy and significance.

...Peace be unto you...(John 20:19).

After Jesus was crucified, the apostles were troubled, hurting, confused, and maybe even questioning their faith. When Jesus appeared to them after His resurrection, He brought peace into their lives by His words and His presence—and He does the same for those of us who seek Him.

People all across our nation and around the world attend church, sing songs, read their Bibles and pray, but they have no joy. Christians who are missing that deep-rooted, deep-seated foundational joy of Jesus have no strength and become like Thomas. They lose hope and forget about God for days; many even give up completely. This could all be avoided if they showed up when Jesus passed by. The first step in attaining peace is simply showing up in His presence. Find a place to get alone with Him. Fear, doubt, depression and loneliness can be eliminated if we are willing to spend time with Jesus.

The other disciples therefore said to him, "We have seen the Lord"(John 20:25).

If, like Thomas, you lack peace and are attempting to find it by reading self-help books or going to counseling, you are settling for secondhand truth. Thomas got the report about Jesus' resurrection and appearance secondhand when he could have experienced it for himself—*but he wasn't there.* He had pulled away from the other apostles. Most of the troubled hearts seeking peace through counseling could find it in just a few minutes in

God's company, listening firsthand to His voice. Peace is His gift to us when we choose to spend time in His presence.

If I don't spend time with God daily, I find myself falling into fear and anxiety. Going even one day without Jesus' presence is sure to cause worry of some kind.

Recently one of my children received a "D" on a big test and all kinds of fear and worry fell on me. That night I had trouble sleeping because I thought my son was failing a class. "It's all my fault; I probably passed this struggle down to him. He's just like his dad."

These thoughts rolled over and over in my mind and I began to think of all the things I could do to remedy the problem—in my own strength. Finally I had exhausted myself both physically and emotionally and I went to where I should have gone in the first place—into God's presence. And that's where I found peace. No, He doesn't always give me the answers right away, but He always gives me peace! I was able to drift off into sleep knowing that God would take care of my son...and me.

Do you need peace? Are you trying to find a good counselor to visit or a good book about peace to read? Don't be like Thomas. Get alone with Jesus and let Him speak directly to your heart, "Peace be with you."

Missing His Mission

...As the Father has sent Me, I also send you (John 20:21).

God gives you peace, and then He gives you a mission, a godly calling for your life. He gives you a sense that your life counts, that He has plans for you, and that you are significant. God stirs you to the place that you awaken every morning with excitement, knowing that He has called you to make a difference. You know you really matter and you're motivated to get involved in His mission for you. You are not called to perform mundane and mediocre tasks. No, He is sending you out with full authority, full power, full love, and full blessing, the same way the Father sent his Son. But you must stay in His presence or the many contradicting voices you hear can confuse you. You will end up worrying about your life, your calling, and your mission. If this happens, don't do anything at all before you get into God's presence.

When Thomas didn't care to show up that day with the apostles, he missed a voice that would have given him a mission—a mission with God's endorsement and empowerment. That would have surely filled him with faith!

I want to encourage you not to even ask Jesus what you are supposed to do with your life; just get in His presence and ask Him to speak to your heart. The mission He has for you will become clear because He will let you know. It is not just a matter of seeking His hand and asking *where He wants you to go* or *what He wants you to do* but seeking the face of God and knowing Him. When you seek His face, His hand will become evident. When you seek the glory of God, all these other things will be added unto you. "Don't worry," Jesus said, "about all these other things. They will take care of themselves."

Missing His Spirit.

And when He had said this, He breathed on them, and said to them, "Receive the Holy Spirit" (John 20:22).

First Jesus gives peace; second, He gives the mission; and third, He gives the Holy Spirit. The fact that Jesus breathed on the apostles implies that He had intimacy with them. He was so close to them that they could feel His breath as He spoke to them. This event symbolically showed the apostles that Jesus would always be near them through the presence of the Holy Spirit. Contrary to what some believe, getting filled with the Spirit is not a one-time event. He calls us into His presence every day to be filled anew. The baptism of the Holy Spirit is a constant flow of His life into our spirit.

Let's look one more time at Thomas: *Now Thomas, called the Twin, one of the twelve, was not with them when Jesus came (John 20:24).*

Are you going to be there when Jesus comes? Are you waiting for Him? Are you seeking Him? Are you asking for Him? Or are you like Thomas?

Aggressive Seeker

Now after the Sabbath, as the first day of the week began to dawn, Mary Magdalene and the other Mary came to see the tomb (Matthew 28:1).

Mary's attitude toward Jesus was completely opposite that of Thomas. There was no doubt in her and no uncertainty about the resurrection. She had probably spent the Sabbath grieving the death of Jesus and praying for God's grace to get through that difficult time. She rose up before dawn the next day to go to the place where Jesus had been buried. She didn't have to go, but she chose to be there, to be present. Waking long before dawn, journeying through the dark into a graveyard, she had to overcome many obstacles. Scriptures do not tell us what she expected to see but she was hungry for Jesus so she continued to seek Him.

Then the disciples went away again to their own homes. But Mary stood...(John 20:10-11).

Not only was Mary the first to arrive at the tomb, she was the last to leave. Peter and the other disciples arrived later than Mary but they went home. Thomas didn't even show up. Contrast the spirits of Mary and Thomas: She was first to arrive and last to leave—he wasn't even motivated to be there. Mary truly wanted more of Jesus.

Mary's persistent seeking for Jesus was similar to Joshua's persistent seeking of *I AM* at the tabernacle in Old Testament times. Joshua stayed at the tabernacle all night seeking God's face because he wanted more of Him. Mary had this same kind of hunger for Jesus.

When you desperately pursue Jesus and are hungry for more of Him, you may not follow set patterns. You may not follow all the rules or be politically correct. You may not wait until Sunday morning to say "hallelujah" or sing worship songs. You can't wait until Sunday—you want to run to Him because you have a heart like Mary's.

Running to Jesus

*But the angel answered and said to the women, "...go
quickly and tell His disciples that He is risen from
the dead, and indeed He is going before you into
Galilee; there you will see Him..." (Matthew 28:5
and 7).*

While Mary was waiting at the tomb she had an amazing encounter with an angel. She saw and heard things
that the others did not. The angel gave her clear and
precise direction where she should go to see Jesus.
Wouldn't you listen to this powerful angel? He told her
to run to the disciples as quickly as possible and not let
anything get her off course.

*So they departed quickly from the tomb with fear
and great joy, and ran to bring His disciples word.
And as they went to tell His disciples, behold, Jesus
met them saying, "Rejoice!" (Matthew 28:8-9)*

The angel told Mary that she and the others could
meet Jesus later in Galilee, but she couldn't wait until the
appointed time. She was supposed to wait but even the
angel couldn't slow her. Protocol didn't matter to her. I
like to think that Mary ran so fast to get to the place
where she would meet Jesus that she overtook Him. The
angel had told her that she would see Him in Galilee, but
she met Him sooner. She seemed to be saying, "I know
you told me to wait, but I can't. I need Jesus *now.*" The
meeting was organized for later but Mary cared little about
organization. She was ready to meet with Jesus. This is

encouraging! It helps me believe that I can have as much of Jesus as I want, whenever I want and as often as I seek Him. He is willing to abide with us but we must draw near to Him.

Never Let Him Go

Mary ignored culturally correct rules and man-made schedules in order to meet Jesus. When she saw Him, she got so excited that she fell on her face, grabbed hold of His feet and would not let Him go. Many of us miss out on many spiritual blessings because we settle for just a little touch of Him from a sermon or during worship time. We are satisfied with a taste of Jesus and neglect to attend the banquet He offers us.

...Lo, I am with you always, even to the end of the age...(Matthew 28:20).

Jesus states that once He has come into your life, you will always be secure and have His companionship. This is not merely a theological principle, however. He also means that He will be with you and *in you* through His Holy Spirit. He will never leave that intimate place with you. When you put your arms around Him, He will not try to pull away. He will sit down and sup with you and commune with you—*and never leave you.*

This concept may seem radical but it is Jesus-style Christianity that He offers to *ordinary* people who want an *extraordinary* walk with Him. Jesus is willing to give us all that we desire of Him. The good news of the resurrection is that we can have fellowship with Him like Mary did. She sought Him early, met Him first, stayed with Him along with the others, and was still standing there when they all had left.

Jesus gives us peace and a mission but above all else He gives us Himself. We don't need riches, fame or comfort, we just need Jesus. As the lyrics of the old hymn state, *"I'd rather have Jesus than silver or gold, I'd rather have Jesus than riches untold...Than to be the king of a vast domain...I'd rather have Jesus than anything..."* [1]

Mary proved that she would rather have Jesus, but Thomas said, "I'll think about it—I'm not quite sure."

What about you? Are you more like Thomas or are you like Mary? Would you rather have Jesus? If so, accept my invitation into a place you've never been before. Come into the presence of Jesus and sit at His feet—begin to really know Him! He loves you more than you can ever imagine and He will meet your every need!

---

[1] *George Beverly Shea, 1922 "I'd Rather Have Jesus"*